Finlay McGill

PHILIP'S STUDENT ATLAS

Published in Great Britain in 2013 by Philip's,
a division of Octopus Publishing Group Limited
(www.octopusbooks.co.uk)
Endeavour House, 189 Shaftesbury Avenue,
London WC2H 8JY
An Hachette UK Company
(www.hachette.co.uk)

Printed in Hong Kong

Cartography by Philip's
Second edition

Copyright © 2013 Philip's

HARDBACK EDITION
ISBN 978-1-84907-282-3

PAPERBACK EDITION
ISBN 978-1-84907-283-0

SUBJECT LIST

Details of other Philip's titles and services can be found on our website at:
www.philips-maps.co.uk

MAP SYMBOLS

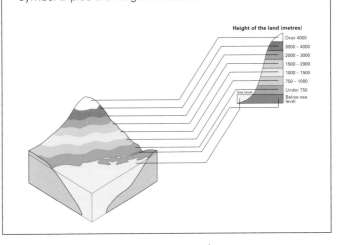

- Sea
- Coastline
- Airport
- Cape name
- Colours showing the height of the land
- Country name
- River
- National boundary (international boundaries are shown as ▭▭▭▭)
- Lake
- Line of longitude
- High point, with height in metres
- River name
- Name of mountain range
- Regional name
- Main railway
- Main road
- Sea feature name
- Line of latitude
- Symbols indicating towns: the larger the population of the town, the larger the symbol

HEIGHT OF LAND

There is an explanation like this one on every page where different colours are used to show the height of the land above sea level.

The highest point in a region is shown with the symbol ▲ plus the height in metres.

Height of the land (metres)

	Over 4000
	3000 – 4000
	2000 – 3000
	1500 – 2000
	1000 – 1500
	750 – 1000
	Under 750
Sea level	
	Below sea level

SCALE BAR

Every map has a scale statement, scale bar and ruler accompanying it. For a full explanation of scale and how to use the scale bar, see page 2.

Scale 1:48 000 000   1 cm on the map = 480 km on the ground

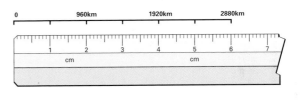

SCALE COMPARISON MAP

This map, or one of the U.K. and Ireland, appears on most of the maps of the continents at the same scale as the main map. They give an idea of the size of that continent.

England and Wales on same scale

LOCATOR MAP

There is a small map such as this on every map page. The bright green area shows how the main map fits into its larger region.

Philip's World Atlases are published in association with The Royal Geographical Society (with The Institute of British Geographers).

The Society was founded in 1830 and given a Royal Charter in 1859 for 'the advancement of geographical science'. Today it is a leading world centre for geographical learning – supporting education, teaching, research and expeditions, and promoting public understanding of the subject.

Further information about the Society and how to join may be found on its website at: **www.rgs.org**

PHOTOGRAPHIC ACKNOWLEDGEMENTS
Alamy /Roger Bamber p. 24 (centre), /Stocktrek Images, Inc. p. 36; **Corbis** /Tim Graham p. 24 (bottom), /Reuters p. 44, /Royalty Free p. 73; **Crown Copyright** p. 7 (map extract); **Eurostar** p. 26; **Fotolia.co.uk** p. 76; **Fugro NPA Ltd** pp. 8, 9, 10, 12, 26, 27, 37, 49, 60, 61, 74, 78, 79; **iStockphoto.com** p. 24 (top); **Patricia and Angus Macdonald** p. 7; **NASA** p. 11; **Precision Terrain Surveys Ltd** p. 6.

TYPES OF SCALE

In this atlas the scale of the map is shown in three ways:

WRITTEN STATEMENT

This tells you how many kilometres on the Earth are represented by one centimetre on the map.

1 cm on the map = 20 km on the ground

SCALE RATIO

This tells you that one unit on the map represents two million of the same unit on the ground.

Scale 1:2 000 000

SCALE BAR

This shows you the scale as a line or bar with a section of ruler beneath it.

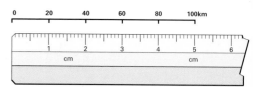

HOW TO MEASURE DISTANCE

The map on the right is a small part of the map of Southern Europe, which is on page 34 in the World section of the atlas.

The scale of the map extract is shown below:

Scale 1:10 000 000   1 cm on the map = 100 km on the ground

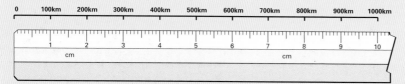

To measure the distance from London to Paris you can use any of the three methods described above.

For example:

USING THE WRITTEN STATEMENT

Using the scale above, you can see that 1 centimetre on the map represents 100 kilometres on the ground.

Measure the distance on the map between London and Paris. You will see that this is about 3.5 centimetres.

If 1 cm = 100 km

then 3.5 cm = 350 km (3.5 x 100)

USING THE SCALE RATIO

Using the scale above, you can see that the ratio is 1:10 000 000.

We know that the distance on the map between the cities is 3.5 cm and we know from the ratio that 1 cm on the map = 10 000 000 cm on the ground.

We multiply the map distance by the ratio.

= 3.5 x 10 000 000 cm
= 35 000 000 cm
= 350 000 m
= 350 km

USING THE SCALE BAR

We know that the distance on the map between the cities is 3.5 centimetres.

Measure 3.5 cm along the scale bar (or use the ruler as a guide) and read off the distance in kilometres.

Using these three methods, now work out the distance between London and Cardiff on the map above.

The map on the left is an extract from the map of Asia on page 39 in the World section of the atlas. Below, you can see the scale of this map. See if you can calculate the distance between Kolkata and Bangkok.

Scale 1:48 000 000   1 cm on the map = 480 km on the ground

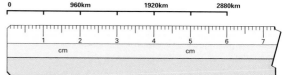

DIFFERENT SIZES OF SCALE

The table on the right shows the distances from London to Paris and Bangkok to Kolkata on the maps on page 2. The map distances are both 3.5 centimetres, but the distances on the ground are very different. This is because the maps are at different scales.

Included on most of the continent maps, in the World section of this

	Map Distance	Map Scale	Distance on the Ground
London – Paris	3.5 centimetres	1:10 000 000	350 kilometres
Bangkok – Kolkata	3.5 centimetres	1:48 000 000	1,680 kilometres

atlas, are **scale comparison maps**. These show you the size of the UK and Ireland, or England and Wales, drawn at the same

scale as the main map on that page. This is to give you an idea of the size of that continent.

Below are three maps which appear in this atlas:

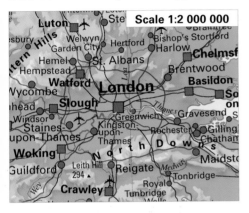

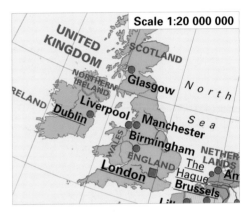

These maps all show London, but the map above shows much more detail than the maps on the right. The map above is a larger-scale map than the maps on the right.

A **large-scale** map shows more detail of a **small** area.

A **small-scale** map shows less detail of a **large** area.

Notice how the scale ratios at the top right of each map are getting larger as the scale of the map gets smaller.

DIRECTION ON THE MAPS

On most of the atlas maps, north is at the top of the page. Lines of latitude cross the maps from east to west. Longitude lines run from south to north. These usually curve a little because the Earth is a globe and not a flat shape.

POINTS OF THE COMPASS

Below is a drawing of the points of a compass. North, east, south and west are called **cardinal points**. Direction is sometimes given in degrees. This is measured clockwise from north. To help you remember the order of the compass points, try to learn this sentence:

Naughty **E**lephants **S**quirt **W**ater

USING A COMPASS

Compasses have a needle with a magnetic tip. The tip is attracted towards the Magnetic North Pole, which is close to the Geographical North Pole. The compass tells you where north is. You can see the Magnetic North Pole on the diagram below.

ACTIVITIES

Look at the map below.
If Ambleside is east of Belfast then:

• Valencia is _____ of Belfast;

• Renfrew is _____ of Ambleside;

• Oxford is _____ of Plymouth;

• Belfast is _____ of Oxford;

• Plymouth is _____ of Renfrew.

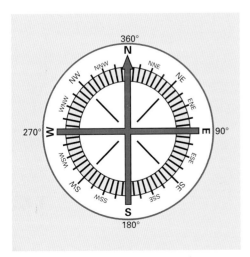

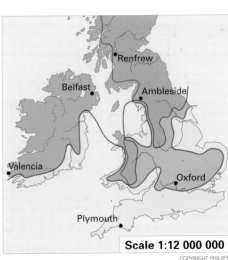

LATITUDE

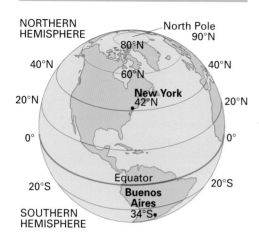

LONGITUDE

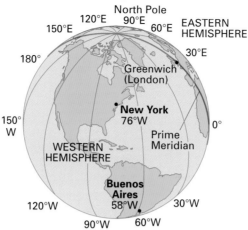

USING LATITUDE & LONGITUDE

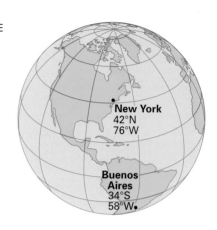

Lines of latitude cross the atlas maps from east to west. The **Equator** is at 0°. All other lines of latitude are either north of the Equator, or south of the Equator. Line 40°N is almost halfway towards the North Pole. The North Pole is at 90°N. At the Equator, a degree of longitude measures about 110 km.

Lines of longitude run from north to south. These lines meet at the North Pole and the South Pole. Longitude 0° passes through Greenwich. This line is also called the Prime Meridian. Lines of longitude are either east of 0° or west of 0°. There are 180 degrees of longitude both east and west of 0°.

There are 60 minutes in a degree. Latitude and longitude lines make a grid. You can find a place if you know its latitude and longitude number. The latitude number is either north or south of the Equator. The longitude number is either east or west of the Greenwich Meridian.

SPECIAL LATITUDE LINES

The Earth's axis is tilted at an angle of approximately 23½°. In June, the northern hemisphere is tilted towards the Sun. On 21 June the Sun is directly overhead at the **Tropic of Cancer**, 23°26′N, and this is midsummer in the northern hemisphere. Midsummer in the southern hemisphere occurs on 21 December, when the Sun is overhead at the **Tropic of Capricorn**, 23°26′S. On the maps in this atlas these are shown as blue dotted lines.

In the North and South Polar regions there are places where the Sun does not rise or set above the horizon at certain times of the year. These places are also shown by a blue dotted line on the maps. The **Arctic Circle** is at 66°34′N and the **Antarctic Circle** is at 66°34′S.

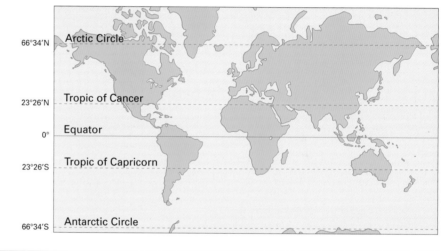

LATITUDE AND LONGITUDE IN THIS ATLAS

In this atlas lines of latitude and longitude are coloured blue.

On large-scale maps, such as those of England and Wales on pages 16–17, there is a line for every degree. On smaller-scale maps only every other, every fifth or even tenth line is shown.

The map on the right shows the UK and Ireland. The latitude and longitude lines are numbered at the edges of the map. The bottom of the map shows whether a place is east or west of Greenwich. The side of the map tells you how far north from the Equator the line is.

Around the edges of the map are small yellow pointers with letters or figures in their boxes. Columns made by longitude lines have letters in their boxes; rows made by latitude lines have figures.

In the index at the end of the atlas, places have figure-letter references as well as latitude and longitude numbers to help you locate the place names on the maps.

On the map opposite, London is in rectangle **8M** (this is where row 8 crosses with column M). Edinburgh is in **4J** and Dublin is in **6F**.

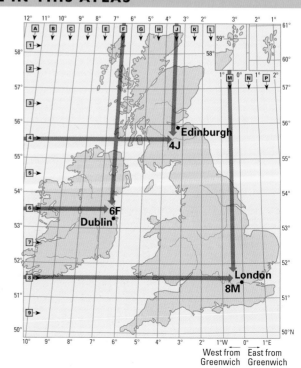

HOW TO FIND A PLACE

The map on the right is an extract from the map of Scotland on page 18. If you want to find Stornoway in the atlas, you must look in the index. Places are listed alphabetically. You will find the following entry:

Stornoway .... 58° 13'N 6° 23'W **18 1B**

The first number in **bold** type is the page number where the map appears. The figure and letter which follow the page number give the grid rectangle on the map in which the feature appears. Here we can see that Stornoway is on page 18 in the rectangle where row 1 crosses column B.

The latitude and longitude number corresponds with the numbered lines on the map. The first set of figures represent the latitude and the second set represent the longitude. The unit of measurement for latitude and longitude is the degree (°) which is divided into minutes (').

Latitude and longitude can be used to locate places more accurately on smaller-scale maps such as those in the World section. A more detailed explanation of how to estimate the minutes can be found on page 90.

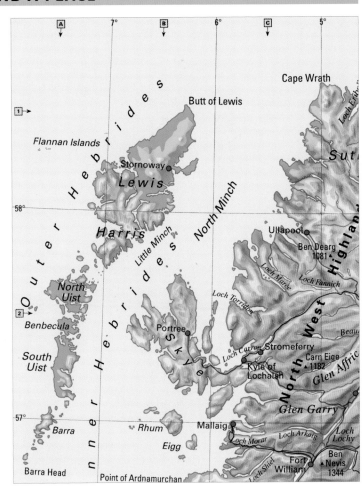

MAKING MAPS

One of the greatest problems in making maps is how to draw the curved surface of the globe on a flat piece of paper. As a globe is three dimensional, it is not possible to show its surface on a flat map without some form of distortion.

This map (right) shows one way of putting the globe on to paper, but because it splits up the land and sea it is not very useful.

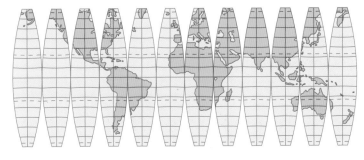

The map below is better because it shows the correct size of places. It is an **equal-area map**. For example, Australia is the correct size in relation to North America, and Europe is the correct size in relation to Africa. Comparing certain areas is a useful way to check the accuracy of maps. Comparing Greenland (2.2 million km²) with Australia (7.7 million km²) is a good 'area test'.

The map below is called **Mercator**. It has been used since the 16th century. The area scale is not equal area, but many sea and air routes are drawn on this type of map because direction is accurate. The scale of distances is difficult to put on a world map. On the Mercator map, scale is correct along the Equator but is less correct towards the Poles.

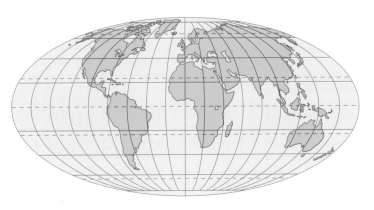

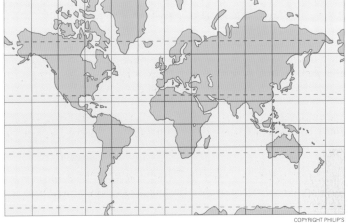

COPYRIGHT PHILIP'S

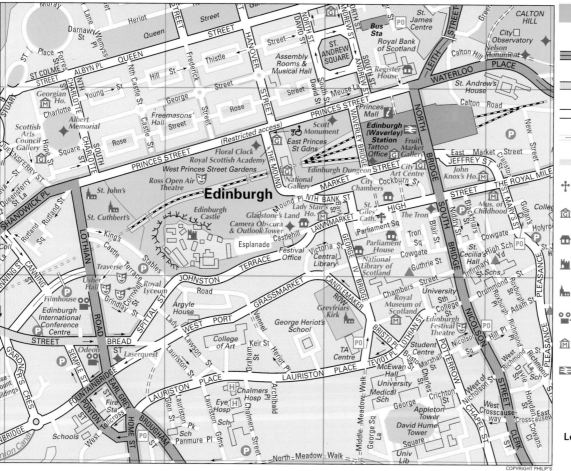

KEY TO MAP SYMBOLS

	Main Road Dual			Shopping Street
	Secondary Road Single			Railway
	Minor Road			Railway / Bus Station
	One Way Street			Shopping Precinct / Retail Park
	Pedestrian Roads			Park
♁	Abbey/Cathedral			Theatre
G	Art Gallery		i	Tourist Information Centre
	Building of Public Interest		✦	Other Place Interest
	Castle		H	Hospital
	Church of interest		P	Parking
	Cinema		PO	Post Office
M	Museum		▲	Youth Hostel
	Railway Station			

Locator map

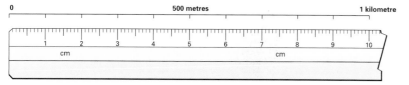

Scale 1:10 000   1 centimetre on the map and aerial photograph = 100 metres on the ground

0   500 metres   1 kilometre

KEY TO MAP SYMBOLS

─30─	Main road	════════	Other road, drive or track, fenced and unfenced
─3074─	Secondary road	··············	Path
	Road generally more than 4m wide	------------	Footpath
	Road generally less than 4m wide	◆────◆	National Trail/ Long Distance Route; Recreation Route
	Single track		Cutting; tunnel; embankment
	Road over; Road under; Level crossing;	●────	Station, open to passengers; siding
	Coniferous trees		Scrub
	non-coniferous trees		Bracken, heath or rough grassland
	Coppice	‖‖‖‖‖‖‖‖‖	Slopes

Place of worship

t or former r worship	┃ with tower ┃ with spire, minaret or dome	CH	Clubhouse
		FB	Footbridge
	Building; important building	PO	Post office
	Lighthouse, disused lighthouse; beacon	Sch	School
	Triangulation pillar; mast	W; Spr	Well; spring

Ground survey height

Air survey height

Surface heights are to the nearest metre above mean sea level. Where two heights are shown, the first height is to the base of the triangulation pillar and the second (in brackets) to the highest natural point of the hill

Vertical face/cliff

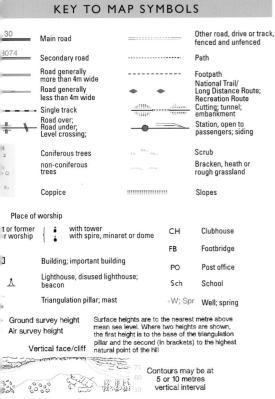

Contours may be at 5 or 10 metres vertical interval

	Parking/Park & Ride, all year/seasonal		Camp site/caravan site
	Information centre, all year/seasonal		Recreation/leisure/ sports centre
	Museum		Golf course or links

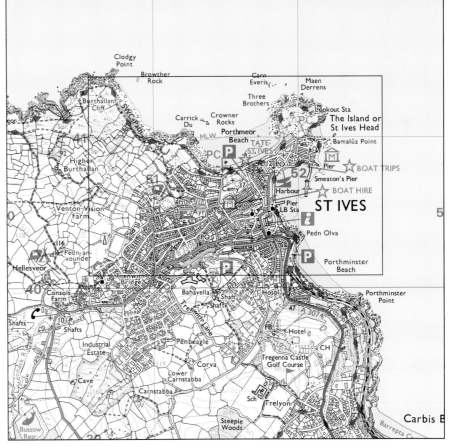

Reproduced from the 2008 Ordnance Survey 1:25,000 Explorer Map with permission of the controller of Her Majesty's Stationery office © Crown Copyright

Scale of photograph 1:10 000

500 metres

centimetre on the photograph = 100 metres on the ground

Scale of map 1:25 000

0	500 metres	1 km	1.5 kilometres

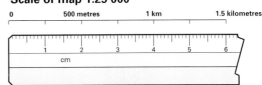

1 centimetre on the map = 250 metres on the ground

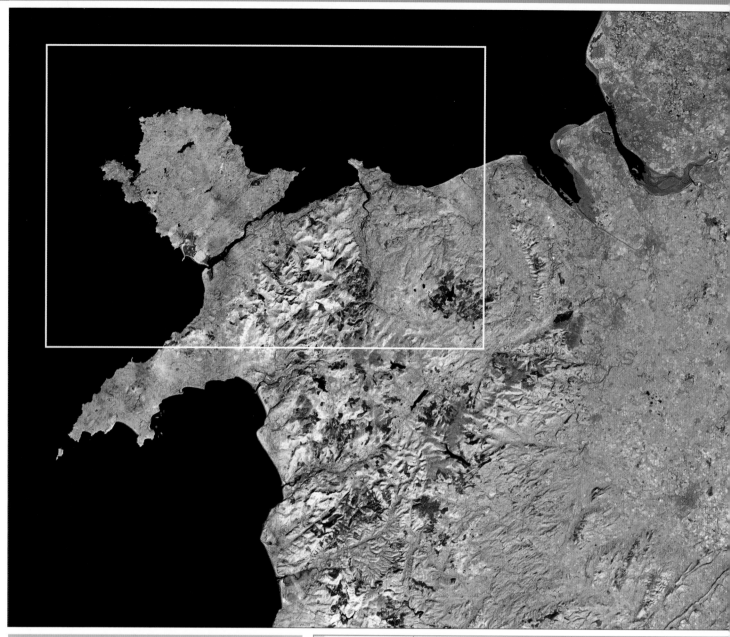

KEY TO MAP SYMBOLS

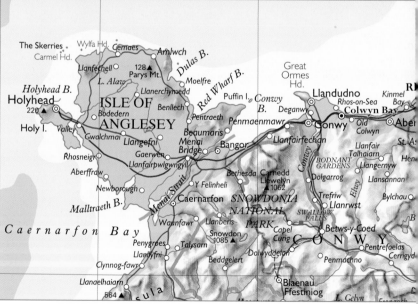

⊙ ⊙ ◉ ◎ ◎ ⊙ ○ ○ Town symbols

Built-up areas

Main passenger railways

CONWY — Administrative area names

Other passenger railways

SNOWDONIA — National park names

⊕ Major airports

Motorways

Rivers

Major roads

Lakes or reservoirs

Other important roads

▲ 1085 Elevations in metres

Administrative boundaries

■ Places of interest

Locator map

Scale 1:760 000 1 cm on the map and satellite image = 7.6 km on the ground

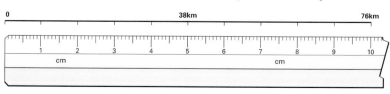

0   38km   76km

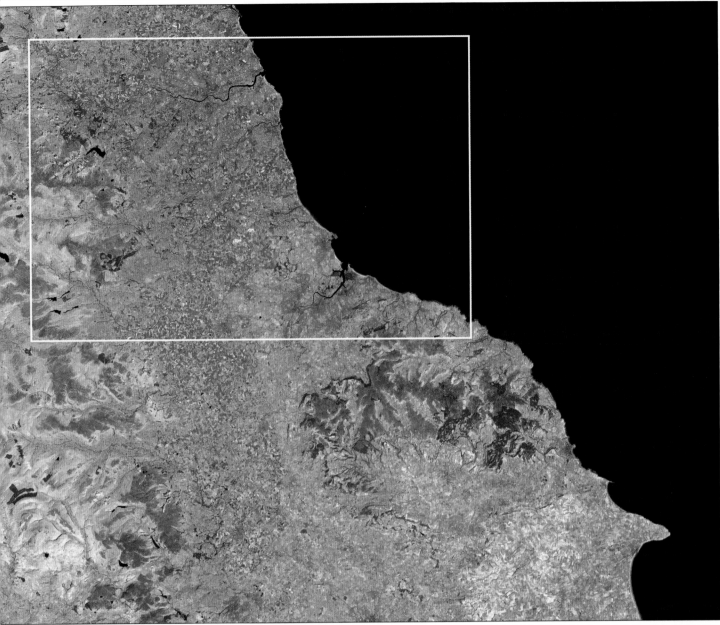

SATELLITE IMAGERY

images on these pages were produced by the
sat 7 satellite, launched by NASA in 1999.
vels around the Earth at a height of over
km. It is able to scan every part of the Earth's
ace once every 16 days. The data is
smitted back to Earth where it is printed in
colours to make certain features stand out.
these pages grass and crops appear light
n, soils and exposed rock light grey, woodland
green, moorland brown, water black and
-up areas dark grey. The image on this page
vs North-east England and the image on page
ows North Wales. Both images were
rded in late March. Comparing the maps,
h are taken from *Philip's Modern School Atlas*
the images helps identify specific features on
mages.

Locator map

COPYRIGHT PHILIP'S

Scale 1:760 000   1 cm on the map and satellite image = 7.6 km on the ground

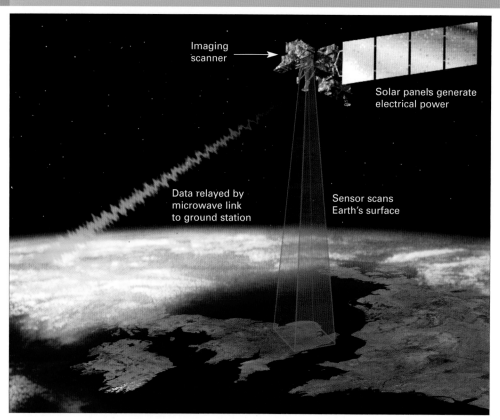

Imaging scanner

Solar panels generate electrical power

Data relayed by microwave link to ground station

Sensor scans Earth's surface

◄ **Earth Observation Satellites**

Powered by outstretched solar panels, Earth Observation Satellites, such as the one shown here, can collect and relay back to Earth huge volumes of geographical data which is then processed and stored on computers.

Depending on the sensors fitted, the choice of orbit and altitude, these satellites can provide detailed imagery of the Earth's surface at close range or monitor environmental issues covering the entire world. Objects as small as 1 metre across can now be seen from space as well as the entire surface of our planet, allowing us to monitor issues such as the atmosphere, land and sea temperature, vegetation, rainfall and ice cover.

The importance of recording this information over time is that it enables us to see long-term changes and increases our understanding of the processes involved. Some satellites have been collecting data for over 25 years. A few of their uses are shown on this page and the page opposite.

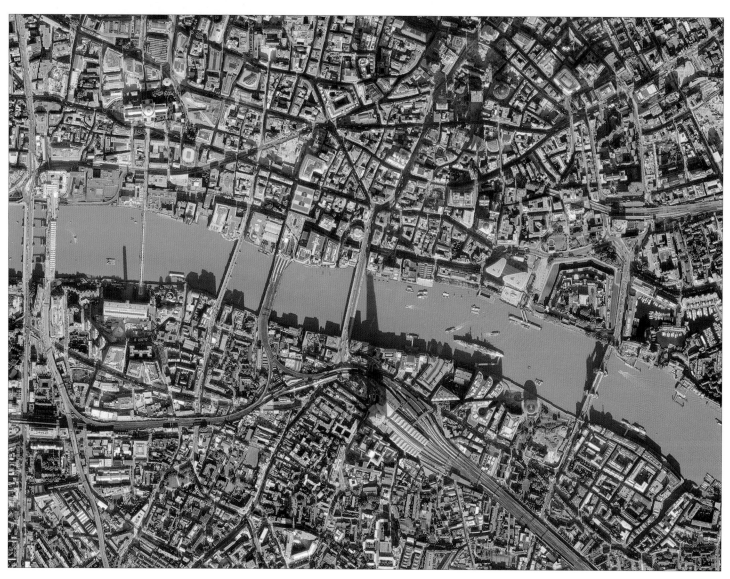

▲ The River Thames, London

This image shows central London from St Paul's Cathedral, in the upper left-hand corner, across to the Tower of London and Tower Bridge on the right-hand side. The image was captured from a satellite 680 km above the Earth and travelling at 6 km per second. It was captured at about midday in late October, the low sun showing clearly the shadows of the Shard and the chimney of Tate Modern. *(Image © EUSI, Inc. All Rights Reserved/Fugro NPA)*

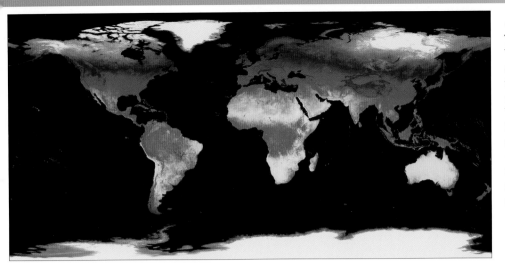

◄ **World Land Surface Temperature, November 2012**
The satellite which captured this data uses another set of sensors that enable it to capture different data and over a much wider area. The colours range from light blue, indicating −25°C, through reds and oranges up to yellow, indicating +45°C. The land surface temperature thus shows the beginning of winter north of the Equator and summer south of the Equator.

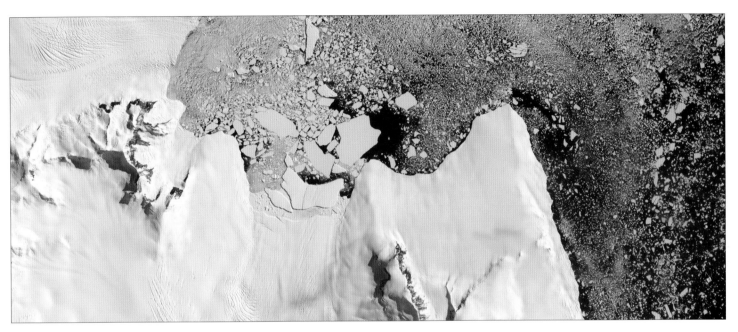

▲ **Ice Cover, Alexander Island, Antarctica**
An important use for satellites is to monitor inaccessible areas of the world that are environmentally sensitive, such as the ice caps surrounding the North and South Poles. This image shows the Hampton Glacier, which is at the foot of the image, flowing towards the sea. The ice then breaks off into a series of icebergs, which can be seen at the top. Because satellites revisit these areas regularly, changes to the extent of the ice can be monitored.

▲ **Weather**
Weather satellites travel at the same speed as the Earth's rotation and stay in daylight to allow them to monitor the same area for major storms and other events. In order to capture as much of the Earth's surface as possible, they orbit farther out in space, about 35,000 km above the Earth's surface. This image clearly shows a hurricane approaching the coast of central America and the Gulf of Mexico.

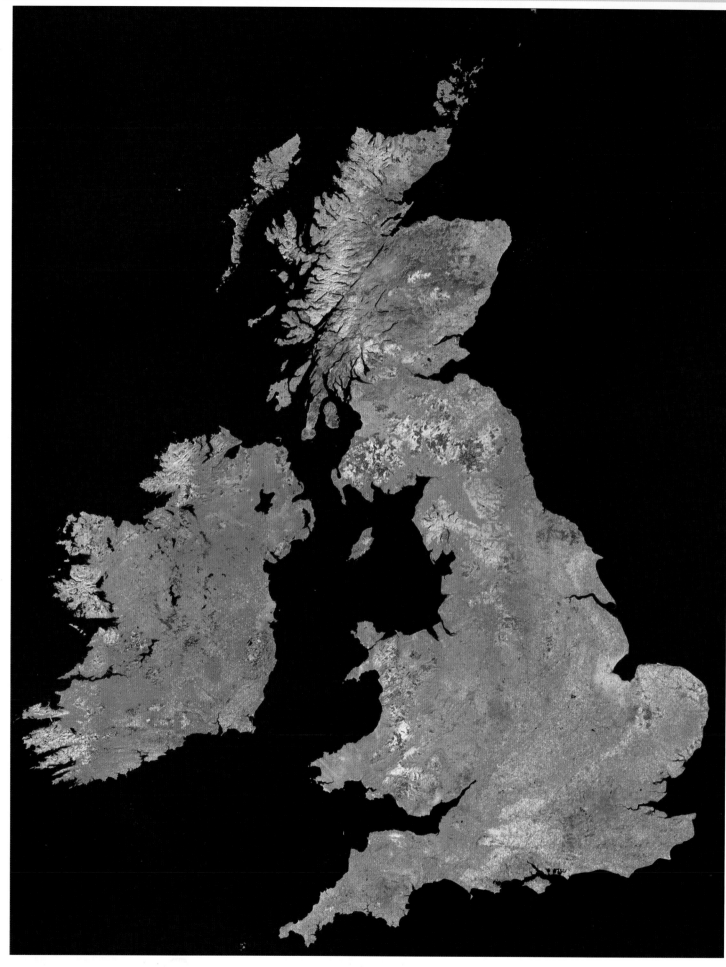

▲ The United Kingdom and Ireland, seen from Space

The colours on this image have been processed to match the natural tone of the landscape. The large amount of agricultural land in the UK is reflected by the extensive green on the image. In Scotland, the snow-covered Cairngorm Mountains can be seen, with brownish-green coniferous forests below the snow line. Most of Ireland has a mid-green colour, which indicates the presence of rich pasture. In the west, the lighter colour indicates moorland or bare rock and is also visible in the Cambrian Mountains in Wales, the Pennines and the Lake District in England, and the Scottish Highlands. Urban areas are shown as dark grey in colour.

Scale 1:4 600 000   1 cm on the map = 46 km on the ground

Height of the land (metres)

over 1000
400-1000
200-400
100-200
0-100
sea level
below sea level

	Highest mountains
	Largest lakes
	Longest rivers

England
Scafell Pike	978m
Windermere	15km²
Thames	346km
Severn	354km

Wales
Snowdon	1085m
Trawsfynydd Lake	5km²
Tywi	109km
Severn	354km

Scotland
Ben Nevis	1344m
Loch Lomond	70km²
Tay	188km

Northern Ireland
Slieve Donard	852m
Lough Neagh	396km²
Bann	128.7km

Ireland
Carrauntoohill	1041m
Lough Corrib	176km²
Shannon	370km

COPYRIGHT PHILIP'S

Scale 1:4 600 000   1 cm on the map = 46 km on the ground

Height of the land (metres)

Over 1000
400 – 1000
200 – 400
Under 200
sea level

Key to map symbols

▴978 Height in metres

International boundaries

LONDON Over 1,000,000 inhabitants

Leeds ● 500,000 – 1,000,000 inhabitants

Plymouth ● 200,000 – 500,000 inhabitants

Oxford ● 100,000 – 200,000 inhabitants

Guildford ● 50,000 – 100,000 inhabitants

Dover • Under 50,000 inhabitants

COPYRIGHT PHILIP'S

COUNTRY FACTS

Country Name	Area (square kilometres)	Inhabitants (thousands 2012)	Capital City or Town
UNITED KINGDOM	**240,883**	**63,047**	**LONDON**
of which England	129,652	52,921	London
Wales	20,628	3,060	Cardiff
Scotland	77,097	5,255	Edinburgh
Northern Ireland	13,532	1,811	Belfast
*Isle of Man	572	84	Douglas
* Jersey	116	98	St. Helier
*Guernsey	63	63	St. Peter Port
IRELAND	**68,896**	**4,722**	**DUBLIN**

* Crown Dependencies which are not part of the U.K.

Scale 1:4 600 000

SCOTLAND
1. ABERDEEN CITY
2. DUNDEE CITY
3. WEST DUNBARTONSHIRE
4. EAST DUNBARTONSHIRE
5. CITY OF GLASGOW
6. INVERCLYDE
7. RENFREWSHIRE
8. EAST RENFREWSHIRE
9. NORTH LANARKSHIRE
10. FALKIRK
11. CLACKMANNANSHIRE
12. WEST LOTHIAN
13. CITY OF EDINBURGH
14. MIDLOTHIAN

WALES
15. SWANSEA
16. NEATH PORT TALBOT
17. BRIDGEND
18. RHONDDA CYNON TAFF
19. MERTHYR TYDFIL
20. CAERPHILLY
21. BLAENAU GWENT
22. TORFAEN
23. CARDIFF
24. NEWPORT

ENGLAND
25. HARTLEPOOL
26. DARLINGTON
27. STOCKTON-ON-TEES
28. MIDDLESBROUGH
29. REDCAR AND CLEVELAND
30. BLACKPOOL
31. BLACKBURN WITH DARWEN
32. HALTON
33. WARRINGTON
34. KINGSTON UPON HULL
35. NORTH EAST LINCOLNSHIRE
36. STOKE-ON-TRENT
37. TELFORD AND WREKIN
38. DERBY CITY
39. CITY OF NOTTINGHAM
40. LEICESTER CITY
41. RUTLAND
42. PETERBOROUGH
43. MILTON KEYNES
44. LUTON
45. NORTH SOMERSET
46. CITY OF BRISTOL
47. BATH AND N. E. SOMERSET
48. SWINDON
49. READING
50. WOKINGHAM
51. WINDSOR AND MAIDENHEAD
52. SLOUGH
53. BRACKNELL FOREST
54. THURROCK
55. SOUTHEND-ON-SEA
56. MEDWAY
57. PLYMOUTH
58. TORBAY
59. POOLE
60. BOURNEMOUTH
61. SOUTHAMPTON
62. PORTSMOUTH
63. BRIGHTON AND HOVE
64. BEDFORD
65. CENTRAL BEDFORDSHIRE

The map shows the 6 counties in Northern Ireland, the 32 unitary authorities in Wales and the 87 unitary authorities in England. Authorities which are too small to name on the map are numbered and listed separately.

Greater London and the 6 English metropolitan counties are coloured white on the map.

Greater London is divided into 32 borough councils and the City of London.

The 6 English metropolitan counties have 36 district councils.

Capital cities

COPYRIGHT PHILIP'S

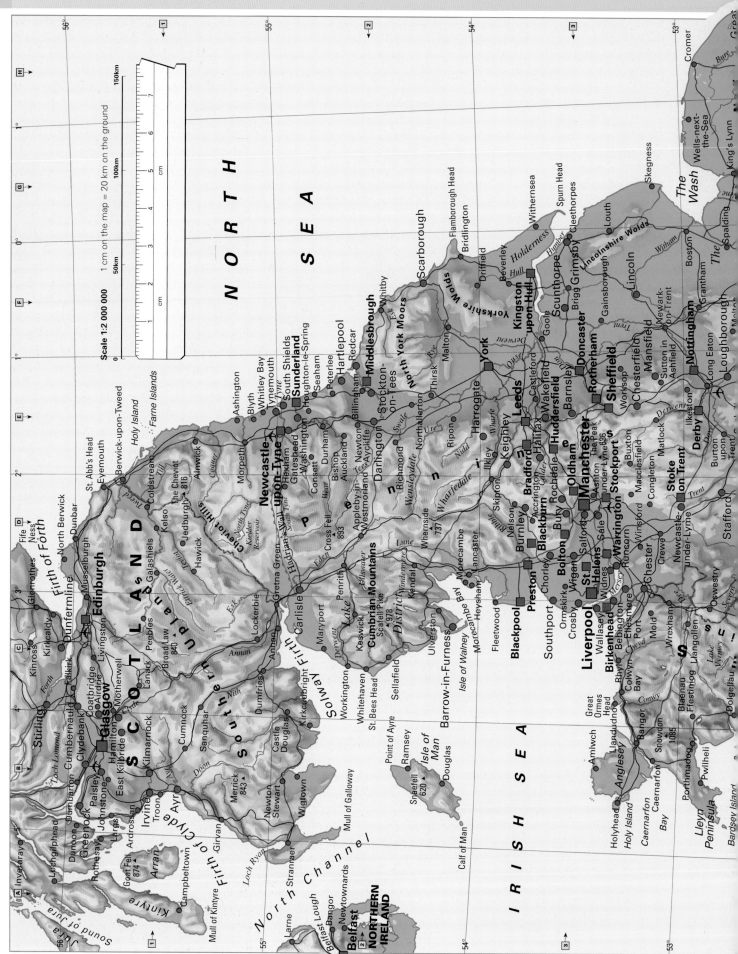

Scale 1:2 000 000

1 cm on the map = 20 km on the ground

0   50km   100km   150km

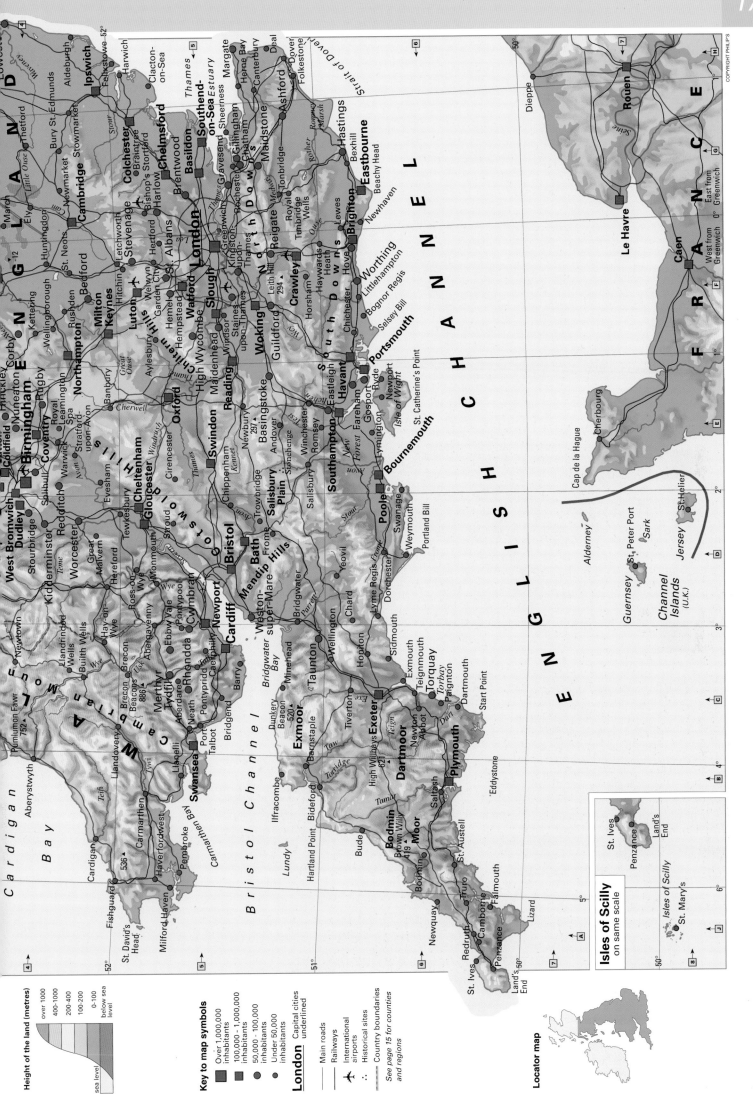

Height of the land (metres)

- over 1000
- 400–1000
- 200–400
- 100–200
- 0–100
- below sea level

sea level

Key to map symbols

- ■ Over 1,000,000 inhabitants
- ■ 100,000 - 1,000,000 inhabitants
- ● 50,000 - 100,000 inhabitants
- ● Under 50,000 inhabitants

London Capital cities underlined

— Main roads
— Railways
✈ International airports
∴ Historical sites
—— Country boundaries

See page 15 for counties and regions

Isles of Scilly
on same scale

St. Ives

Penzance

Land's End

Isles of Scilly

St. Mary's

Locator map

COPYRIGHT PHILIP'S

Orkney Islands
on same scale

Shetland Islands
on same scale

Locator map

Scale 1:2 000 000   1 cm on the map = 20 km on the ground

0   50km   100km   150km   200km

COPYRIGHT PHILIP'S

ATLANTIC OCEAN

NORTHERN IRELAND

Ulster

IRELAND

CONNAUGHT

LEINSTER

MUNSTER

IRISH SEA

CELTIC SEA

SCOTLAND

WALES

St. George's Channel

North Channel

Donegal Bay

Galway Bay

Dundalk Bay

Dublin

Belfast

Cork

Height of the land (metres)

over 1000
400-1000
200-400
100-200
0-100
below sea level
sea level

Key to map symbols

Over 1,000,000 inhabitants
100,000 - 1,000,000 inhabitants
50,000 - 100,000 inhabitants
Under 50,000 inhabitants

Dublin Capital cities underlined

Scale 1:2 000 000

Main roads
Railways
International airports
Country boundaries

See page 15 for counties and regions

Locator map

West from Greenwich

COPYRIGHT PHILIP'S

Weather is measured in terms of rainfall, temperature, cloudiness, sunshine and wind over a short period of time, usually less than a day. Climate is the average of the weather over a longer period, usually 30 years.

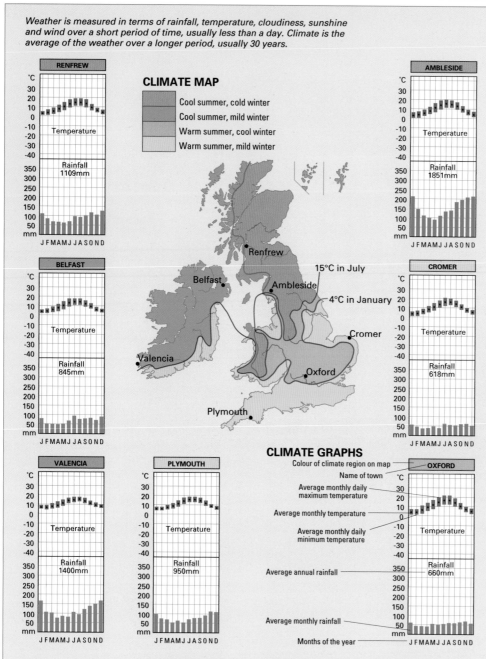

CLIMATE MAP

Cool summer, cold winter
Cool summer, mild winter
Warm summer, cool winter
Warm summer, mild winter

RENFREW
Temperature
Rainfall 1109mm

AMBLESIDE
Temperature
Rainfall 1851mm

BELFAST
Temperature
Rainfall 845mm

CROMER
Temperature
Rainfall 618mm

VALENCIA
Temperature
Rainfall 1400mm

PLYMOUTH
Temperature
Rainfall 950mm

OXFORD
Temperature
Rainfall 660mm

15°C in July
4°C in January

CLIMATE GRAPHS
Colour of climate region on map
Name of town
Average monthly daily maximum temperature
Average monthly temperature
Average monthly daily minimum temperature
Average annual rainfall
Average monthly rainfall
Months of the year

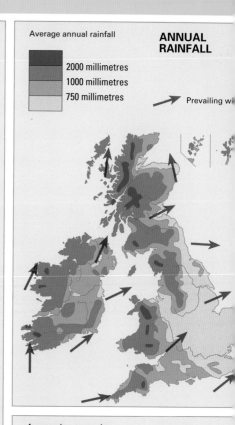

Average annual rainfall

ANNUAL RAINFALL

2000 millimetres
1000 millimetres
750 millimetres

Prevailing wi

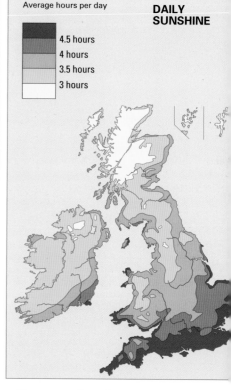

Average hours per day

DAILY SUNSHINE

4.5 hours
4 hours
3.5 hours
3 hours

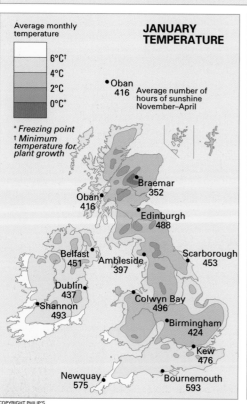

Average monthly temperature

JANUARY TEMPERATURE

6°C †
4°C
2°C
0°C *

* Freezing point
† Minimum temperature for plant growth

Oban 416   Average number of hours of sunshine November–April

Braemar 352
Oban 416
Edinburgh 488
Belfast 451
Ambleside 397
Scarborough 453
Dublin 437
Shannon 493
Colwyn Bay 496
Birmingham 424
Kew 476
Newquay 575
Bournemouth 593

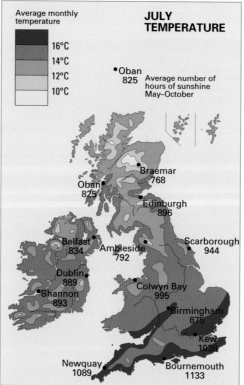

Average monthly temperature

JULY TEMPERATURE

16°C
14°C
12°C
10°C

Oban 825   Average number of hours of sunshine May–October

Braemar 768
Oban 825
Edinburgh 896
Belfast 834
Ambleside 792
Scarborough 944
Dublin 889
Shannon 893
Colwyn Bay 995
Birmingham 875
Kew 1038
Newquay 1089
Bournemouth 1133

Temperature Records
Highest
38.5°C Brogdale near Faversham, (Kent) 10 August 2003
Lowest
-27.2°C Braemar, Aberdeenshire, 10 January 1982 and
11 February 1895, Altnaharra, Highland, 30 December 1995

Rainfall Records
Highest 24 hour total
279 mm Martinstown, near Dorchester, Dorset, 18 July 195
The highest total for any 24 hour period is 316mm at
Seathwaite, Cumbria on 19 November 2009.

Sunshine Records
Highest monthly total
390 hours Eastbourne and Hastings, Sussex, July 1911
Lowest monthly total
0 hours Westminster, Greater London, December 1890

Winds (highest gusts)
150 knots Cairngorm, 20 March 1986

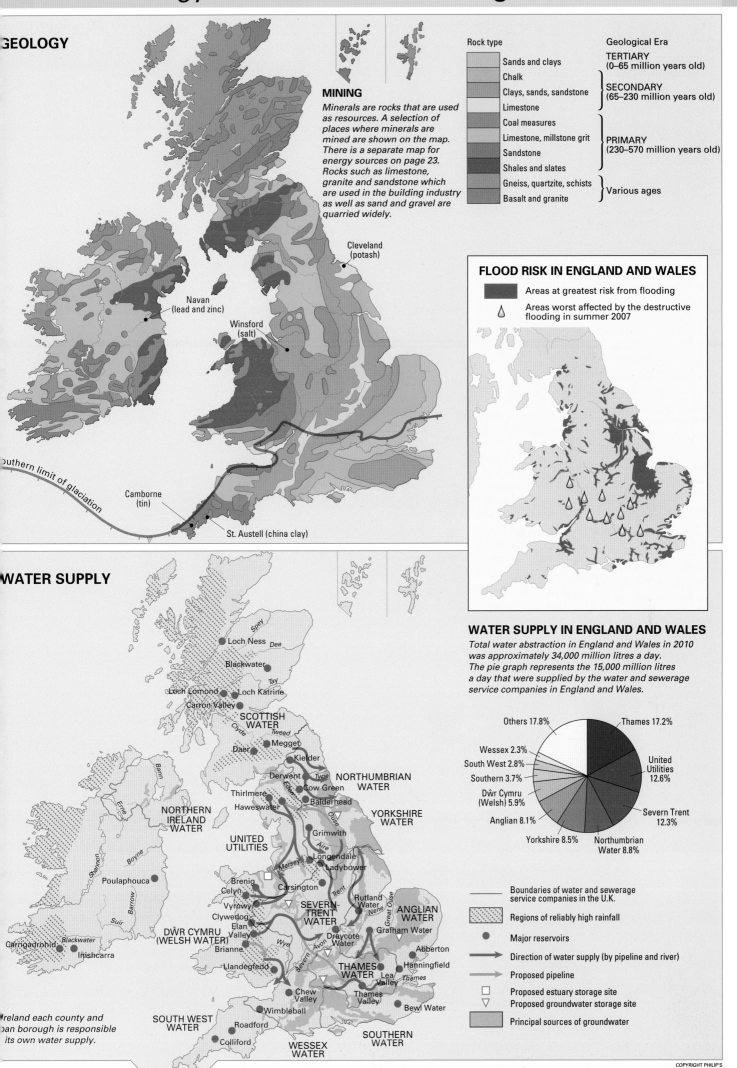

GEOLOGY

MINING

Minerals are rocks that are used as resources. A selection of places where minerals are mined are shown on the map. There is a separate map for energy sources on page 23. Rocks such as limestone, granite and sandstone which are used in the building industry as well as sand and gravel are quarried widely.

Rock type — **Geological Era**

Rock type	Era
Sands and clays	TERTIARY (0–65 million years old)
Chalk	
Clays, sands, sandstone	SECONDARY (65–230 million years old)
Limestone	
Coal measures	
Limestone, millstone grit	PRIMARY (230–570 million years old)
Sandstone	
Shales and slates	
Gneiss, quartzite, schists	Various ages
Basalt and granite	

Cleveland (potash)

Navan (lead and zinc)

Winsford (salt)

Southern limit of glaciation

Camborne (tin)

St. Austell (china clay)

FLOOD RISK IN ENGLAND AND WALES

- Areas at greatest risk from flooding
- Areas worst affected by the destructive flooding in summer 2007

WATER SUPPLY

Spey
Loch Ness   Dee
Blackwater
Tay
Loch Lomond   Loch Katrine
Carron Valley
SCOTTISH WATER
Clyde
Tweed
Daer   Megget
Kielder
Derwent   Tyne   NORTHUMBRIAN WATER
Cow Green
Thirlmere   Eden   Balderhead
Haweswater   YORKSHIRE WATER
Ouse
NORTHERN IRELAND WATER
Grimwith
UNITED UTILITIES   Aire
Longendale
Mersey   Ladybower
Poulaphouca
Brenig   Trent
Celyn   Carsington
Vyrnwy   SEVERN-   Rutland Water
Clywedog   TRENT   Nene   ANGLIAN
Elan   WATER   Great Ouse   WATER
DŴR CYMRU   Valley   Grafham Water
(WELSH WATER)   Draycote
Brianne   Wye   Water
Avon   Abberton
Llandegfedd   THAMES   Hanningfield
Severn   WATER   Lea   Thames
Valley
Chew   Thames Valley
Valley   Bewl Water
Wimbleball
SOUTH WEST   Roadford
WATER   SOUTHERN
Colliford   WATER
WESSEX WATER

Carrigadrohid   Blackwater
Inishcarra

Bann
Erne
Shannon
Boyne
Barrow
Suir

In Ireland each county and urban borough is responsible for its own water supply.

WATER SUPPLY IN ENGLAND AND WALES

Total water abstraction in England and Wales in 2010 was approximately 34,000 million litres a day. The pie graph represents the 15,000 million litres a day that were supplied by the water and sewerage service companies in England and Wales.

- Others 17.8%
- Thames 17.2%
- Wessex 2.3%
- United Utilities 12.6%
- South West 2.8%
- Southern 3.7%
- Dŵr Cymru (Welsh) 5.9%
- Severn Trent 12.3%
- Anglian 8.1%
- Yorkshire 8.5%
- Northumbrian Water 8.8%

— Boundaries of water and sewerage service companies in the U.K.

Regions of reliably high rainfall

● Major reservoirs

→ Direction of water supply (by pipeline and river)

→ Proposed pipeline

□ Proposed estuary storage site

▽ Proposed groundwater storage site

Principal sources of groundwater

COPYRIGHT PHILIP'S

TYPES OF FARM

- Dairy cattle
- Beef cattle
- Sheep
- Pigs and/or poultry
- Mixed farming
- Market gardening (fruit and vegetables)
- Cereals
- Other crops (mainly potatoes, sugar beet)
- Northern limit of 9 month growing season
- Forests
- Built-up areas

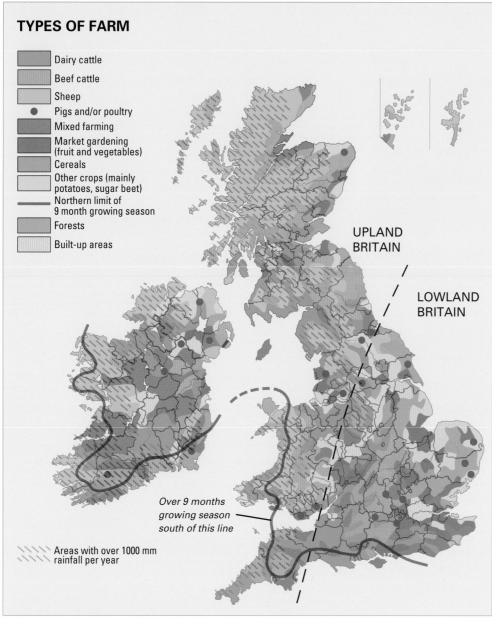

UPLAND BRITAIN

LOWLAND BRITAIN

Over 9 months growing season south of this line

Areas with over 1000 mm rainfall per year

CEREAL FARMING

The percentage of the total farmland used for growing cereals

- Over 40%
- 30 – 40%
- 20 – 30%
- 10 – 20%
- 0 – 10%

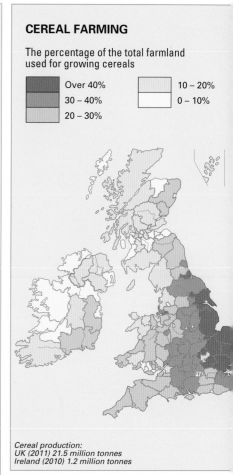

Cereal production:
UK (2011) 21.5 million tonnes
Ireland (2010) 1.2 million tonnes

DAIRY FARMING

The number of dairy cows per 100 hectares of farmland

- Over 40
- 30 – 40
- 20 – 30
- 10 – 20
- 0 – 10

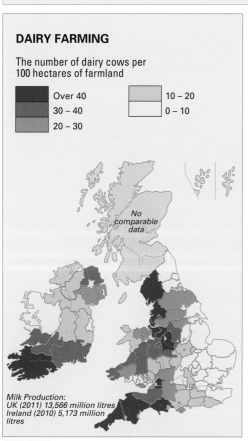

No comparable data

Milk Production:
UK (2011) 13,566 million litres
Ireland (2010) 5,173 million litres

LIVESTOCK FARMING

The number of beef cattle, sheep and pigs per 100 hectares of farmland

- Over 400
- 300 – 400
- 200 – 300
- 100 – 200
- Under 100

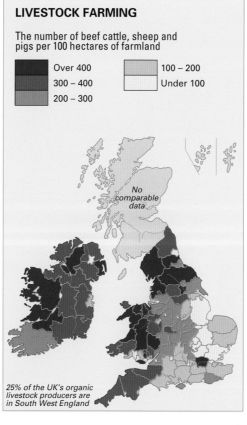

No comparable data

25% of the UK's organic livestock producers are in South West England

Scalloway   Lerw

Scrabster

Kinlochbervie

West Coast of Scotland 366,569 tonnes   Ullapool   Fraserburgh

Mallaig   Peterhe

North Sea 295,367 ton

Killybegs   Kirkcudbright

Portavogie

Kilkeel   Ardglass

Rossaveel

Howth   Holyhead   Penrhyn

Dunmore East

Castletown Bearhaven   Milford Haven

Bristol Channel and Celtic Sea 25,384 tonnes   Shoreham

Brixham   Newha

Newlyn   Plymouth

English Channel 49,507 tonnes

West Ireland and Sole Bank 34,378 tonnes

FISHING

Major fishing ports by size of catch landed

The most importar inshore fishing gro

- Mainly deep sea fish (e.g. cod)
- Mainly shallow sea fish (e.g. mackerel)
- Mainly shellfish e.g. lobster

North Sea 295,367 tonnes

Total amount caught i each fishing region 201

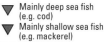
1000 500 200 100 50 m   Depth of sea in metres

COPYRIGHT PHILIP'S

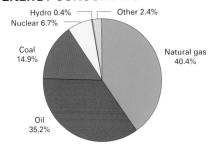

ENERGY CONSUMPTION BY FUEL

Hydro 0.4%
Other 2.4%
Nuclear 6.7%
Coal 14.9%
Natural gas 40.4%
Oil 35.2%

Total U.K. consumption in 2010:
209.1 million tonnes of oil equivalent

CHANGES IN ELECTRICITY GENERATION

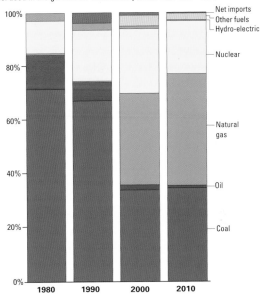

Fuel used in the generation of electricity in the U.K. 1980 – 2010

Net imports
Other fuels
Hydro-electric
Nuclear
Natural gas
Oil
Coal

100% 80% 60% 40% 20% 0%
1980 1990 2000 2010

RENEWABLE ENERGY

The amount of energy generated from renewable sources in kilowatt hours, 2010

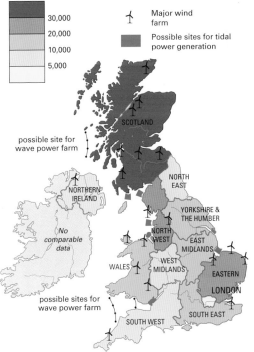

30,000
20,000
10,000
5,000

Major wind farm

Possible sites for tidal power generation

possible site for wave power farm

SCOTLAND

NORTH EAST

NORTHERN IRELAND

YORKSHIRE & THE HUMBER

No comparable data

NORTH WEST

EAST MIDLANDS

WALES

WEST MIDLANDS

EASTERN

LONDON

possible sites for wave power farm

SOUTH WEST

SOUTH EAST

ENERGY SOURCES

- ▬ Coalfield
- ● Coal-fired power station
- ▬ Peat-cutting area in Ireland
- ● Peat-fired power station
- ▲▲ Oilfield
- ─ Oil pipeline (with terminal)
- ● Oil-fired power station
- ▲▲ Gasfield
- ─ Gas pipeline (with terminal)
- ● Gas-fired power station
- ● Coal, biomass & gas-fired power station
- ● Hydro-electric power station
- ○ Nuclear power station
- *Only major power stations and fields are shown*
- ─ International dividing line

ENERGY IMPORTS

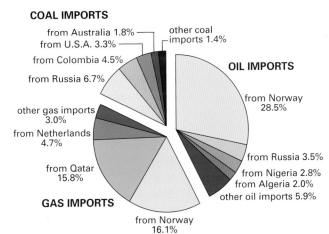

COAL IMPORTS

from Australia 1.8%
from U.S.A. 3.3%
from Colombia 4.5%
from Russia 6.7%
other coal imports 1.4%

OIL IMPORTS

from Norway 28.5%
from Russia 3.5%
from Nigeria 2.8%
from Algeria 2.0%
other oil imports 5.9%

other gas imports 3.0%
from Netherlands 4.7%
from Qatar 15.8%

GAS IMPORTS

from Norway 16.1%

Total U.K. imports 2011 125.6 million tonnes of oil equivalent

CHANGES TO COAL MINING IN THE U.K.

	1960	1980	2010
Production (million tonnes)	195	126	18
Number of employees (thousands)	631	297	9
Number of deep mines	698	211	12

COPYRIGHT PHILIP'S

Numbers employed

CHANGES IN EMPLOYMENT IN THE U.K.

Employment by industry

- Services
- Transport
- Manufacturing
- Mining & energy supply
- Agriculture, forestry & fishing

▲ Canary Wharf, London, is a centre of banking important part of the service industry.

▲ These Mini Clubman cars are being manufactured at the BMW factory, Oxford.

▲ An engineer is shown working on a jet engine in the Rolls-Royce factory, Derby.

INCOME

The average gross weekly earnings of males and females in full employment in 2010

- Over £600
- £550 – £600
- £500 – £550
- £450 – £500
- £400 – £450
- Under £400

No comparable data

Average weekly earnings (2010) U.K. £499 Ireland €684

EMPLOYMENT IN SERVICES

The percentage of the workforce employed in the service industry in 2010

- Over 85%
- 80 – 85%
- 75 – 80%
- 70 – 75%
- Under 70%

EMPLOYMENT IN MANUFACTURING INDUSTRY

The percentage of the workforce employed in manufacturing in 2010

- Over 20%
- 16% – 20%
- 14% – 16%
- 12% – 14%
- 10% – 12%
- Under 10%

UNEMPLOYMENT

The percentage of the workforce unemployed in 2010

- Over 12%
- 10% – 12%
- 8% – 10%
- 6% – 8%
- 4% – 6%
- Under 4%

U.K. TRADE

Trade is balanced by money coming in for service such as banking and insurance.

Total Imports 2010 $558.6 billion

- Food and drink 9.1%
- Other goods 5.6%
- Machinery and transport equipment 31.3%
- Manufactured goods 27.6%
- Fuel, chemicals and minerals 26.4%

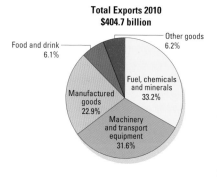

Total Exports 2010 $404.7 billion

- Food and drink 6.1%
- Other goods 6.2%
- Fuel, chemicals and minerals 33.2%
- Machinery and transport equipment 31.6%
- Manufactured goods 22.9%

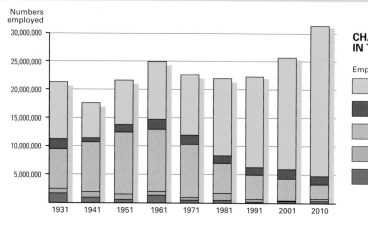
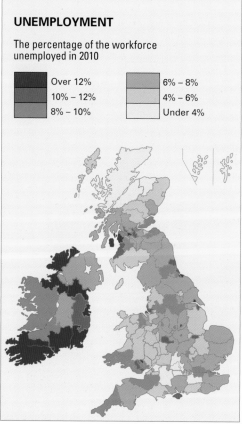
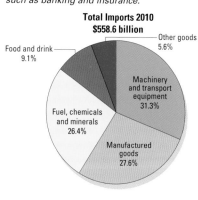

POPULATION FACTS

U.K. Population 2012	63,047,000
of which England	52,921,000
Scotland	5,255,000
Wales	3,060,000
Northern Ireland	1,811,000
Ireland Population 2012	**4,722,000**

AGE STRUCTURE OF THE U.K. IN 1901 AND 2010

he age structure shows how old people are and the
ercentage in each age group that is male and female.
ch diagram is called a population pyramid. For example,
1901, 20% of the female population was aged between
–19. In 2010, about 12% were in this group.

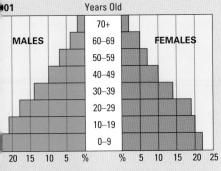

01   Years Old

MALES   FEMALES

70+
60–69
50–59
40–49
30–39
20–29
10–19
0–9

20 15 10 5 %   % 5 10 15 20 25

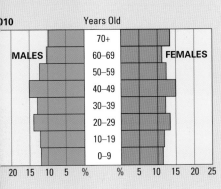

010   Years Old

MALES   FEMALES

70+
60–69
50–59
40–49
30–39
20–29
10–19
0–9

20 15 10 5 %   % 5 10 15 20 25

POPULATION DENSITY

Number of people per square kilometre in 2011

- Over 1000
- 500 – 1000
- 200 – 500
- 100 – 200
- 50 – 100
- 25 – 50
- Under 25

The average density for the U.K. is 261 people per km².

The average density for Ireland is 67 people per km².

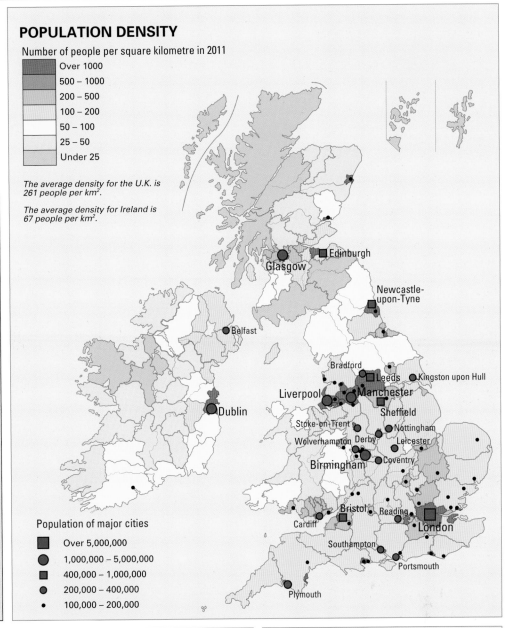

Population of major cities

- ■ Over 5,000,000
- ● 1,000,000 – 5,000,000
- ■ 400,000 – 1,000,000
- ● 200,000 – 400,000
- • 100,000 – 200,000

ETHNIC GROUPS

thnic minorities as a % of total population
1 2010

- Over 25%
- 10 – 25%
- 5 – 10%
- 0 – 5%

thnic minority groups

38 000 Total number of
ethnic minority
people in each
region

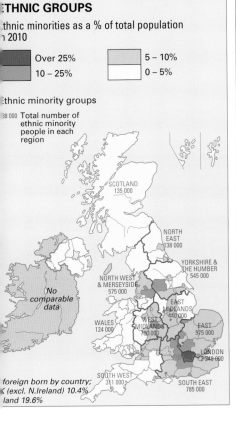

SCOTLAND
135 000

NORTH
EAST
138 000

YORKSHIRE &
THE HUMBER
545 000

NORTH WEST
& MERSEYSIDE
575 000

EAST
MIDLANDS
440 000

*No
comparable
data*

WALES
124 000

WEST
MIDLANDS
780 000

EAST
575 000

LONDON
2 348 000

SOUTH WEST
311 000

SOUTH EAST
785 000

foreign born by country;
(excl. N.Ireland) 10.4%
land 19.6%

YOUNG PEOPLE

The percentage of the population under
15 years old in 2010

- Over 22%
- 20 – 22%
- 18 – 20%
- 16 – 18%
- 14 – 16%

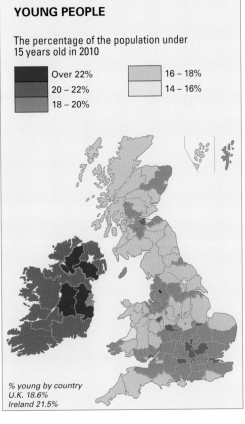

% young by country
U.K. 18.6%
Ireland 21.5%

OLD PEOPLE

The percentage of the population over
pensionable age in 2010

- Over 22%
- 20 – 22%
- 18 – 20%
- 16 – 18%
- 14 – 16%
- Under 14%

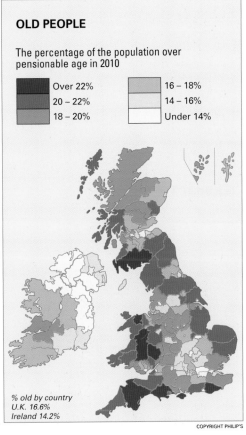

% old by country
U.K. 16.6%
Ireland 14.2%

ROADS AND FERRIES

- M6 Motorways
- Other main roads
- Principal car ferry routes

Scrabster, Stornoway, Wick, Kirkwall, Lerwick, Ullapool, Invergordon, Inverness, Aberdeen, Oban, Perth, Dundee, Glasgow, Edinburgh, Troon, Derry/Londonderry, Newcastle, Larne, Carlisle, Stranraer, Belfast, Sligo, Douglas, Morecambe, Dundalk, Fleetwood, Leeds, Hull, Galway, Liverpool, Manchester, Sheffield, Dublin, Dún Laoghaire, Holyhead, Limerick, Shrewsbury, Leicester, Norwich, Killarney, Cork, Waterford, Rosslare, Birmingham, Cambridge, Fishguard, Harwich, Felixstowe, Pembroke, Swansea, Oxford, London, Cardiff, Bristol, Ramsgate, Dunkirk, Exeter, Southampton, Poole, Portsmouth, Folkestone, Dover, Plymouth, Weymouth, Newhaven, Calais, Penzance, Boulogne

RAILWAYS

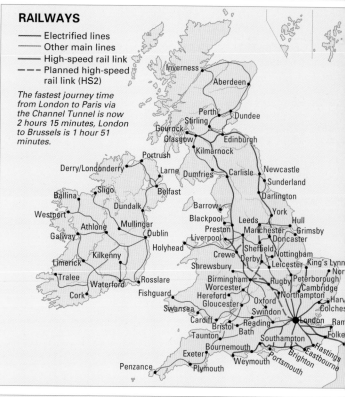

- Electrified lines
- Other main lines
- High-speed rail link
- Planned high-speed rail link (HS2)

The fastest journey time from London to Paris via the Channel Tunnel is now 2 hours 15 minutes, London to Brussels is 1 hour 51 minutes.

Inverness, Aberdeen, Perth, Dundee, Stirling, Gourock, Glasgow, Edinburgh, Kilmarnock, Portrush, Derry/Londonderry, Larne, Dumfries, Carlisle, Newcastle, Sunderland, Ballina, Sligo, Belfast, Darlington, Westport, Dundalk, Barrow, York, Athlone, Mullingar, Blackpool, Preston, Leeds, Hull, Galway, Dublin, Liverpool, Manchester, Grimsby, Doncaster, Kilkenny, Holyhead, Crewe, Sheffield, Nottingham, Limerick, Derby, Leicester, King's Lynn, Tralee, Shrewsbury, Birmingham, Rugby, Peterborough, Waterford, Rosslare, Worcester, Northampton, Cambridge, Cork, Fishguard, Hereford, Oxford, Swansea, Gloucester, Swindon, Colchester, Cardiff, Bristol, Reading, London, Taunton, Bath, Southampton, Folkestone, Exeter, Bournemouth, Brighton, Hastings, Penzance, Weymouth, Portsmouth, Eastbourne, Plymouth

AIRPORTS

Passenger traffic in thousands (2010)

60,000
30,000
5,000
1,000

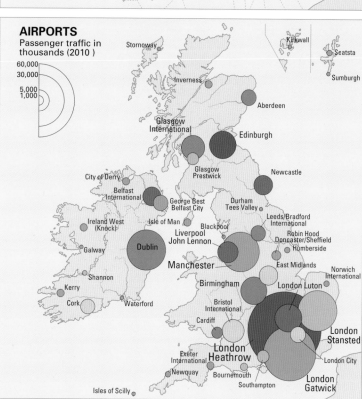

Stornoway, Kirkwall, Seatsa, Inverness, Sumburgh, Aberdeen, Glasgow International, Edinburgh, Glasgow Prestwick, Newcastle, City of Derry, Belfast International, George Best Belfast City, Durham Tees Valley, Ireland West (Knock), Isle of Man, Leeds/Bradford International, Galway, Blackpool, Liverpool John Lennon, Robin Hood Doncaster/Sheffield, Dublin, Humberside, Shannon, Manchester, East Midlands, Kerry, Birmingham, Norwich International, Cork, Waterford, London Luton, Bristol International, Cardiff, London Stansted, Exeter International, London Heathrow, London City, Newquay, Bournemouth, London Gatwick, Isles of Scilly, Southampton

SEAPORTS

Goods traffic by port in thousand tonnes (2010)

50,000
25,000
10,000
5,000

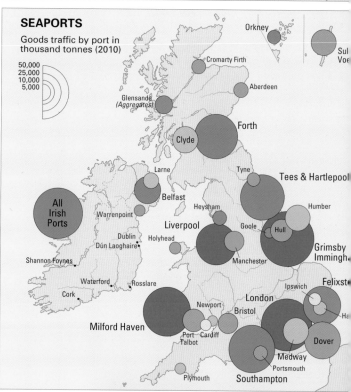

Orkney, Sul Voe, Cromarty Firth, Aberdeen, Glensanda (Aggregates), Forth, Clyde, Larne, Tyne, Tees & Hartlepool, All Irish Ports, Belfast, Heysham, Humber, Warrenpoint, Liverpool, Goole, Hull, Dublin, Holyhead, Manchester, Grimsby Immingham, Dún Laoghaire, Shannon Foynes, Waterford, Rosslare, Ipswich, Felixstowe, Cork, Newport, London, Bristol, Milford Haven, Port Talbot, Cardiff, Dover, Medway, Portsmouth, Plymouth, Southampton

TOURIST TRAFFIC

Millions of visitors from U.K. (2010)

0　1　2　3　4　5　6　7　8　9　10

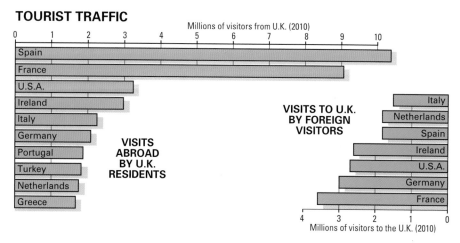

VISITS ABROAD BY U.K. RESIDENTS

- Spain
- France
- U.S.A.
- Ireland
- Italy
- Germany
- Portugal
- Turkey
- Netherlands
- Greece

VISITS TO U.K. BY FOREIGN VISITORS

- Italy
- Netherlands
- Spain
- Ireland
- U.S.A.
- Germany
- France

4　3　2　1　0
Millions of visitors to the U.K. (2010)

▲ Eurostar at St. Pancras International. This station is the London terminus of the high-speed rail link to Europe, High Speed 1.

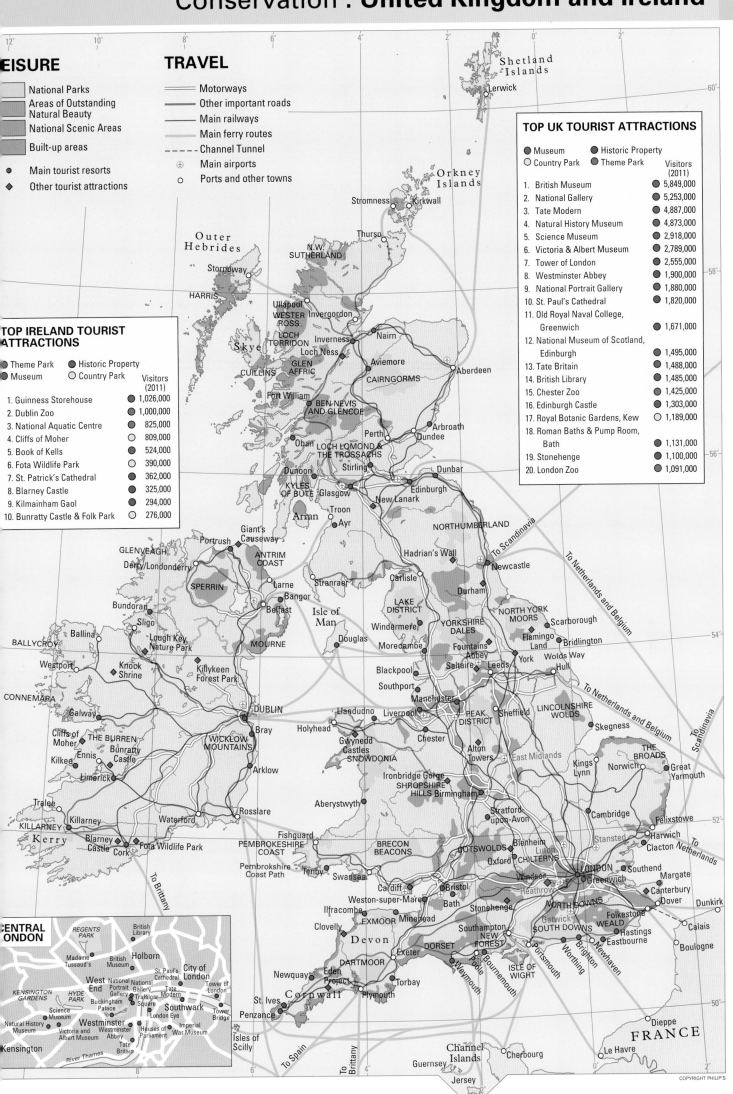

LEISURE

- National Parks
- Areas of Outstanding Natural Beauty
- National Scenic Areas
- Built-up areas

- ● Main tourist resorts
- ◆ Other tourist attractions

TRAVEL

- Motorways
- Other important roads
- Main railways
- Main ferry routes
- – – – Channel Tunnel
- ✈ Main airports
- ○ Ports and other towns

TOP UK TOURIST ATTRACTIONS

- ● Museum
- ● Historic Property
- ○ Country Park
- ● Theme Park

		Visitors (2011)
1.	British Museum ●	5,849,000
2.	National Gallery ●	5,253,000
3.	Tate Modern ●	4,887,000
4.	Natural History Museum ●	4,873,000
5.	Science Museum ●	2,918,000
6.	Victoria & Albert Museum ●	2,789,000
7.	Tower of London ●	2,555,000
8.	Westminster Abbey ●	1,900,000
9.	National Portrait Gallery ●	1,880,000
10.	St. Paul's Cathedral ●	1,820,000
11.	Old Royal Naval College, Greenwich ●	1,671,000
12.	National Museum of Scotland, Edinburgh ●	1,495,000
13.	Tate Britain ●	1,488,000
14.	British Library ●	1,485,000
15.	Chester Zoo ●	1,425,000
16.	Edinburgh Castle ●	1,303,000
17.	Royal Botanic Gardens, Kew ○	1,189,000
18.	Roman Baths & Pump Room, Bath ●	1,131,000
19.	Stonehenge ●	1,100,000
20.	London Zoo ●	1,091,000

TOP IRELAND TOURIST ATTRACTIONS

- ● Theme Park
- ● Historic Property
- ● Museum
- ○ Country Park

		Visitors (2011)
1.	Guinness Storehouse ●	1,026,000
2.	Dublin Zoo ●	1,000,000
3.	National Aquatic Centre ●	825,000
4.	Cliffs of Moher ○	809,000
5.	Book of Kells ●	524,000
6.	Fota Wildlife Park ○	390,000
7.	St. Patrick's Cathedral ●	362,000
8.	Blarney Castle ●	325,000
9.	Kilmainham Gaol ●	294,000
10.	Bunratty Castle & Folk Park ○	276,000

COPYRIGHT PHILIP'S

COPYRIGHT PHILIP'S

Ural Mountains

Ob

Ural

Volga

Caspian Sea

Volga Uplands

Don

Volga

Caucasus

Elbrus 5642

Ararat 5165

Tigris

Euphrates

A S I A

Northern Dvina

Central Russian Uplands

Dnieper

Black Sea

Anatolia

Bosporus

Cyprus

White Sea

Lake Onega

Lake Ladoga

Carpathians

Danube

Balkans

Aegean Sea

Crimea

Crete

Lapland

North Cape

Torne

Gulf of Finland

Gulf of Bothnia

Baltic Sea

North European Plain

Vistula

Danube

Dinaric Alps

Adriatic Sea

Apennines

Po

Sicily

Oder

Elbe

Norwegian Sea

Faroe Islands

Shetland Islands

Orkney Islands

British Isles

North Sea

Great Britain

Rhine

Mont Blanc 4808

Rhône

Corsica

Sardinia

Balearic Islands

Iceland

Ireland

English Channel

Seine

Loire

Bay of Biscay

Pyrenees

Ebro

Tagus

Cape Finisterre

Iberian Peninsula

Strait of Gibraltar

Cape St. Vincent

MEDITERRANEAN SEA

A F R I C A

ATLANTIC OCEAN

Arctic Circle

Scandinavia

A L P S

Scale 1:20 000 000

East from Greenwich

Height of the land
(metres)

over 4000
2000 – 4000
1000 – 2000
400 – 1000
200 – 400
0 – 200
below sea level

sea level

Locator map

Arctic Ocean
Asia
Mediterranean Sea
Africa
Atlantic Ocean
North America

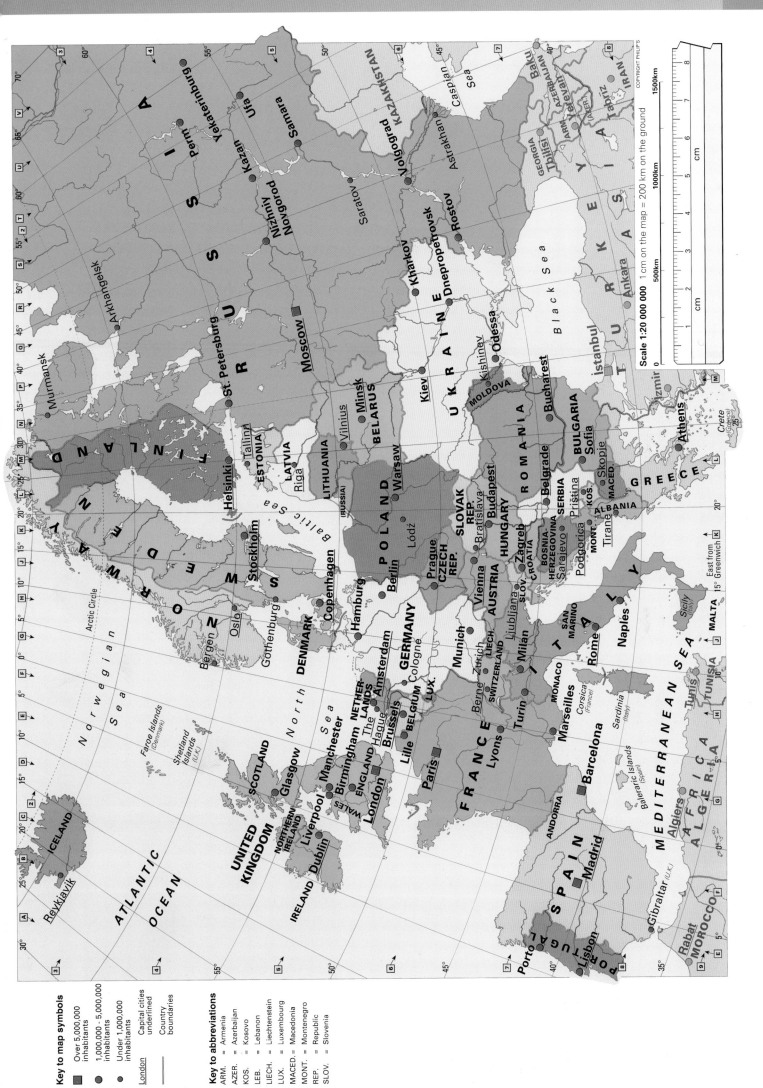

Key to map symbols

- ■ Over 5,000,000 inhabitants
- ● 1,000,000 - 5,000,000 inhabitants
- • Under 1,000,000 inhabitants

London Capital cities underlined

—— Country boundaries

Key to abbreviations

ARM. = Armenia
AZER. = Azerbaijan
KOS. = Kosovo
LEB. = Lebanon
LIECH. = Liechtenstein
LUX. = Luxembourg
MACED. = Macedonia
MONT. = Montenegro
REP. = Republic
SLOV. = Slovenia

Scale 1:20 000 000 1 cm on the map = 200 km on the ground
1 cm on the map = 200 km on the ground

COPYRIGHT PHILIP'S

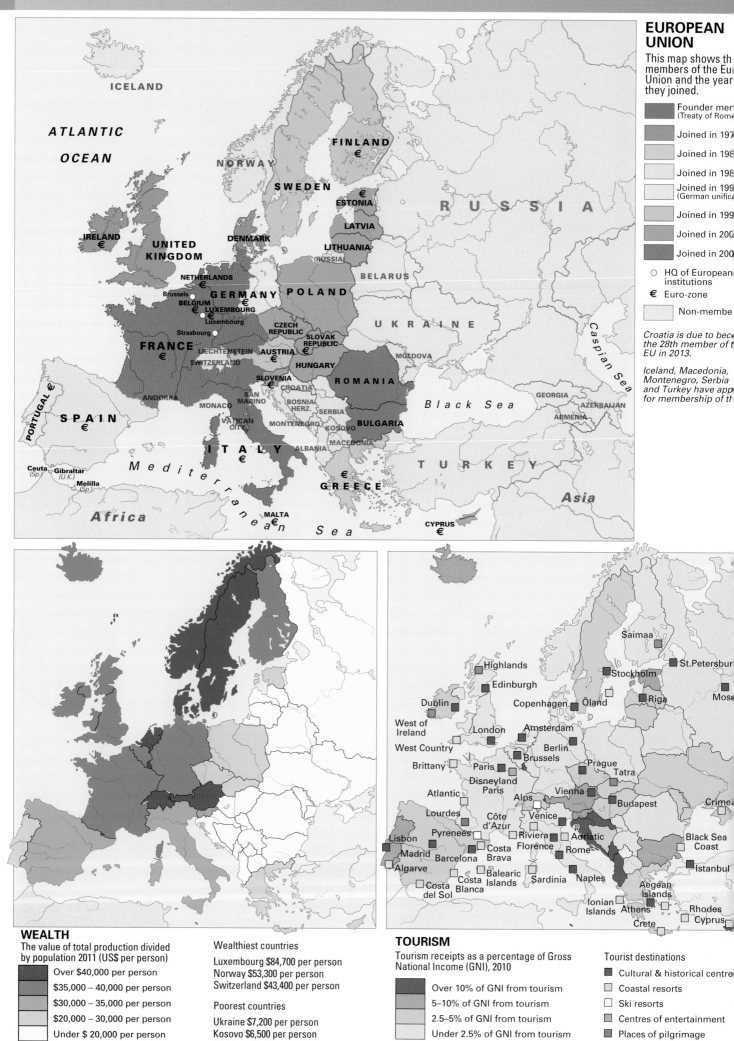

EUROPEAN UNION

This map shows th members of the Eu Union and the year they joined.

Founder mer (Treaty of Rome)

Joined in 197

Joined in 198

Joined in 198

Joined in 199 (German unifica

Joined in 199

Joined in 200

Joined in 200

○ HQ of European institutions

€ Euro-zone

Non-membe

Croatia is due to bec the 28th member of t EU in 2013.

Iceland, Macedonia, Montenegro, Serbia and Turkey have app for membership of th

WEALTH

The value of total production divided by population 2011 (US$ per person)

Over $40,000 per person

$35,000 – 40,000 per person

$30,000 – 35,000 per person

$20,000 – 30,000 per person

Under $ 20,000 per person

UK $35,900 per person

Wealthiest countries

Luxembourg $84,700 per person
Norway $53,300 per person
Switzerland $43,400 per person

Poorest countries

Ukraine $7,200 per person
Kosovo $6,500 per person
Moldova $3,400 per person

TOURISM

Tourism receipts as a percentage of Gross National Income (GNI), 2010

Over 10% of GNI from tourism

5–10% of GNI from tourism

2.5–5% of GNI from tourism

Under 2.5% of GNI from tourism

Tourist destinations

■ Cultural & historical centre
□ Coastal resorts
□ Ski resorts
■ Centres of entertainment
■ Places of pilgrimage
■ Places of great natural bea

Scale 1:10 000 000   1 cm on the map = 100 km on the ground

0   100km 200km 300km 400km 500km 600km

COPYRIGHT PHILIP'S

Height of the land (metres)

over 4000
2000-4000
1000-2000
400-1000
200-400
0-200
sea level
below sea level

Key to map symbols

■ Over 5,000,000 inhabitants

● 1,000,000 - 5,000,000 inhabitants

• Under 1,000,000 inhabitants

Helsinki Capital cities underlined

Country boundaries

Locator map

Height of the land (metres)

over 4000
2000-4000
1000-2000
400-1000
200-400
0-200
below sea level

sea level

Key to map symbols

● Over 5,000,000 inhabitants

● 1,000,000 - 5,000,000 inhabitants

● Under 1,000,000 inhabitants

Paris Capital cities underlined

— — Country boundaries

Locator map

SWEDEN
Sundsvall
Uppsala
Gävle
Västerås
Örebro
Norrköping
Karlstad
Linköping
Östersund
Västerdal
Jönköping
Borås
Gothenburg
Götaland
Lake Vättern
Lake Vänern
Glåma
Lillehammer
Gålhøpiggen 2469
Jotunheimen
NORWAY
Oslo
Drammen
Frederikstad
Kristiansand
Lindesnes
Skagerrak
Skagen
Jutland
Aalborg
DENMARK
Esbjerg
Odense
Aarhus
Sjaelland
Copenhagen
Helsingborg
Malmö
Kattegat
Bornholm (Denmark)
Baltic Sea
Rügen
Szczecin
POLAND
Oder
Neisse
Potsdam
Berlin
Magdeburg
Brunswick
Göttingen
Halle
Leipzig
Dresden
Prague
CZECH REP.
Chemnitz
Erfurt
Kassel
GERMANY
Frankfurt
Main
Koblenz
Bonn
Cologne
Dortmund
Essen
Düsseldorf
Münster
Osnabrück
Bielefeld
Hanover
Weser
Bremen
Oldenburg
Hamburg
Lübeck
Kiel
Kiel Canal
Flensburg
Fehmarn
Lolland
Rostock
Elbe
Rhine
Arnhem
Groningen
Frisian Islands
NETHERLANDS
Amsterdam
Utrecht
The Hague
Rotterdam
Ghent
Antwerp
Brussels
BELGIUM
Lille
Boulogne
Calais
Dover

Kristiansund
Ålesund
Florø
Bergen
Stavanger
Sogne Fjord
Hardanger Fjord
Norwegian Sea
ATLANTIC OCEAN
Torshavn
Faroe Islands (Denmark)
St. Kilda (U.K.)
Shetland Islands (U.K.)
Lerwick
Kirkwall
Orkney Islands
Wick
Cape Wrath
Stornoway
Lewis
Hebrides
Skye
Mull
Inverness
Loch Ness
Ben Nevis 1344
SCOTLAND
Aberdeen
Dundee
Edinburgh
Glasgow
Carlisle
Newcastle
Middlesbrough
UNITED KINGDOM
Leeds
Sheffield
Nottingham
Leicester
Birmingham
ENGLAND
Oxford
London
Thames
Southampton
Portsmouth
Isle of Wight
Bournemouth
Plymouth
Land's End
Penzance
Cape Clear
Celtic Sea
St. George's Channel
Swansea
Cardiff
Severn
Snowdon 1085
WALES
Bristol
Isle of Man
Douglas
Irish Sea
Liverpool
Manchester
Belfast
NORTHERN IRELAND
Londonderry
Derry
IRELAND
Dublin
Sligo
Galway
Achill Island
Shannon
Limerick
Waterford
Cork
North Sea
Norwich
The Wash

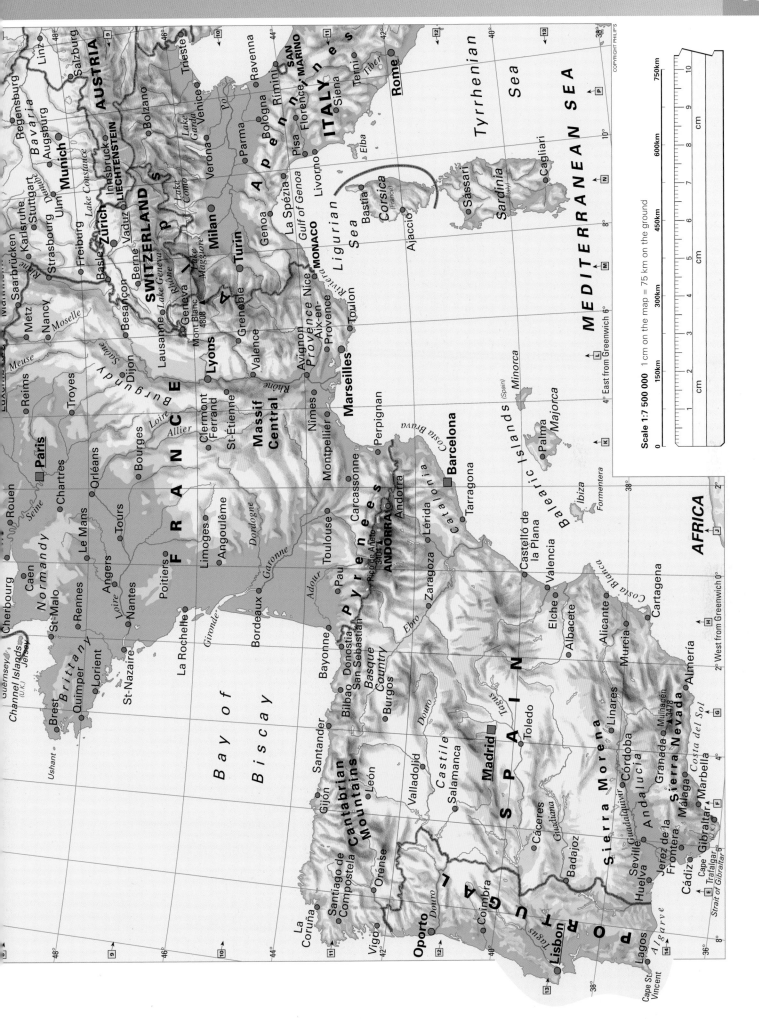

Scale 1:7 500 000 1 cm on the map = 75 km on the ground

4° East from Greenwich 6°

MEDITERRANEAN SEA

Tyrrhenian Sea

Ligurian Sea

AFRICA

2° West from Greenwich 0°

ATLANTIC
OCEAN

IRELAND
WALES
ENGLAND
Birmingham
Cardiff
Bristol
Plymouth
Thames
London
English Channel
Channel Islands (U.K.)
NETHERLANDS
The Hague
Amsterdam
Rotterdam
Antwerp
BELGIUM
Lille
Brussels
Bonn
LUXEMBOURG
Luxembourg
Le Havre
Brest
Paris
Seine
Rennes
Nancy
Strasbourg
Nantes
Orléans
Tours
Dijon
FRANCE
Limoges
Clermont Ferrand
Lyons
St. Etienne
Massif Central
Bordeaux
Garonne
Grenoble
Toulouse
Montpellier
MONACO
Nice
Marseilles
Toulon
Riviera

Hamburg
Szczec
Bremen
Berlin
Hanover
GERMANY
Dortmund
Cologne
Leipzig
Dresden
Frankfurt
Mannheim
Prague
Nuremberg
CZEC
Stuttgart
Danube
Munich
Linz
Basle
Zürich
Berne
LIECHTENSTEIN
AUSTR
SWITZERLAND
Lake Geneva
Geneva
Mont Blanc 4808
Milan
Turin
Verona
Venice
Po
Parma
Genoa
Bologna
Rímini
SAN MARINO
Florence
Pisa
Siena
Gran Sasso 2914
Ljubli
SLOVEN
Tries
Adriati

Bay of Biscay

La Coruña
Gijón
Santander
Vigo
Cantabrian Mountains
León
Bilbao
Burgos
Oporto
Douro
PORTUGAL
Salamanca
Valladolid
Deuro
Pyrenees
Pic d'Aneto 3404
ANDORRA
Zaragoza
Ebro
Catalonia
Costa Brava
Barcelona
Madrid
Tagus
SPAIN
Toledo
Tagus
Lisbon
Badajoz
Guadiana
Sierra Morena
Guadalquivir
Seville
Cordoba
Algarve
Cádiz
Granada
Mulhacén 3478
Málaga
Almeria
Costa del Sol
Tangier
Gibraltar (U.K.)
Strait of Gibraltar
Ceuta (Spain)
Tétouan
Melilla (Spain)
Oran
Mostaganem
Algiers
Blida
Valencia
Costa Blanca
Alicante
Murcia
Cartagena
Balearic Islands (Spain)
Palma
Ibiza
Majorca
Minorca

Corsica (France)
Ajaccio
Rome
ITAL
Mount Vesu
Naples
Pompeii
Sardinia (Italy)
Cágliari
Tyrrhenian Sea
Strómb
Palermo
Etna 3340
Sicily
Catá

MEDITERRANEAN

Bizerte
Annaba
Bejaïa
Tunis
Carthage
Constantine
Sousse
Valletta
MALTA
ALGERIA
Atlas Mountains
Biskra
Chott Melrhir
TUNISIA
Chott Djerid
Sfax
Djerba
MOROCCO
Fès
Ifrane
Oujda
AFRICA
Sahara Desert
Tripoli
Al Aziziyah
LIBYA

50°
45°
40°
35°
30°
10°
5°
0°
5°
10°
West from Greenwich
East from Greenwich

Height of the land (metres)
over 4000
2000-4000
1000-2000
400-1000
200-400
0-200
sea level
below sea level

Key to map symbols
Over 5,000,000 inhabitants
1,000,000 - 5,000,000 inhabitants
Under 1,000,000 inhabitants
Sofia Capital cities underlined
Country boundaries
Historical sites   Seasonal lakes

Scale 1:10 000 000   1 cm on the map = 100 km on the ground
0   250km   500km   750km   1000km

cm   1   2   3   4   5   6   7   8   9   10
cm   cm   cm

Cross-section along latitude 45°N

Locator map

COPYRIGHT PHILIP'S

Map labels

SWITZERLAND
LIECHTENSTEIN
AUSTRIA
SLOVENIA
CROATIA
FRANCE

A l p s
Dolomites
Bolzano
3342
Trento
Mont Blanc 46 4808
Monte Rosa 4634
Lake Maggiore
Lake Como
Lake Garda
Udine
Trieste
Milan
Brescia
Bergamo
Vicenza
Verona
Padua
Venice
Novara
Turin
Piacenza
Parma
Réggio
Ferrara
Alessandria
Módena
Bologna
Po
Riviera
Genoa
Forlì
Ravenna
Gulf of Genoa
La Spézia
SAN MARINO
Rímini
A p e n n i n e s
San Remo
MONACO
Pisa
Florence
Adriatic Sea
Ligurian Sea
Livorno
Siena
Ancona
Corsica (France)
Elba
Grosseto
Perúgia
Terni ▲2912
Pescara
Tiber
Celano
Strait of Bonifacio
VATICAN CITY
Rome
Fóggia
Sássari
Ólbia
Latina
Bari
Mount Vesuvius 1281
Naples
Pompeii
Bríndisi
Sardinia (Italy)
1834 ▲
Ischia
Capri
Salerno
Sorrento
Potenza
Táranto
Lecce
Gulf of Táranto
Tyrrhenian Sea
Cágliari
Cosenza ▲1928
Ionian Sea
Strait of Otranto
Strómboli ▲924
Aeolian Islands
Égadi Islands
Palermo
Messina
Réggio di Calabria
Marsala
Mount Etna 3323
Sicily
Catánia
Pantelleria
Siracusa
East from Greenwich

Locator map

▲ **Strómboli** Known as the 'Lighthouse of the Mediterranean', it is one of three active volcanoes in Italy. The others are Mount Etna and Mount Vesuvius

Scale 1:6 250 000   1 cm on the map = 62.5 km on the ground

0   62.5km   125km   187.5km   250km   312.5km   375km

cm   1   2   3   4   5   6

Key to map symbols

- ■ Over 1,000,000 inhabitants
- ● 500,000 – 1,000,000 inhabitants
- • Under 500,000 inhabitants
- **Rome** Capital cities
- —— Country boundaries
- ∴ Historical site

Height of the land (metres)

- over 4000
- 2000-4000
- 1000-2000
- 400-1000
- 200-400
- 0-200 (sea level)
- below sea level

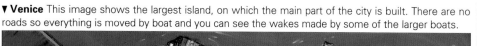

▼ **Venice** This image shows the largest island, on which the main part of the city is built. There are no roads so everything is moved by boat and you can see the wakes made by some of the larger boats.

REGION

ALTO ADIGE TRENTINO
VALLE D'AOSTA
FRIULI-VENEZIA GIULA
LOMBARDY
VENETO
PIEDMONT
EMILIA-ROMAGNA
LIGURIA
TUSCANY
MARCHE
UMBRIA
ABRUZZO
LAZIO
MOLISE
SARDINIA
CAMPANIA
PUGLIA
BASILICATA
CALABRIA
SICILY

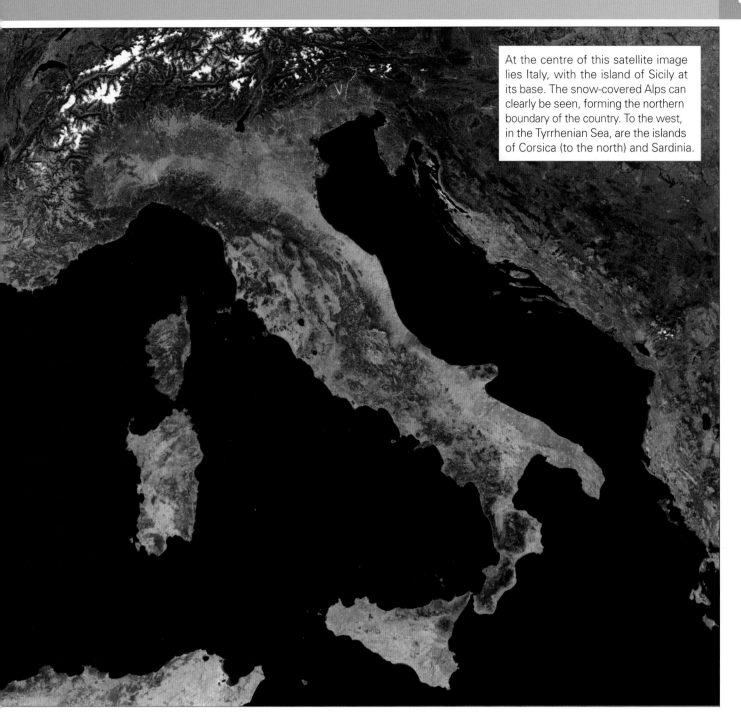

At the centre of this satellite image lies Italy, with the island of Sicily at its base. The snow-covered Alps can clearly be seen, forming the northern boundary of the country. To the west, in the Tyrrhenian Sea, are the islands of Corsica (to the north) and Sardinia.

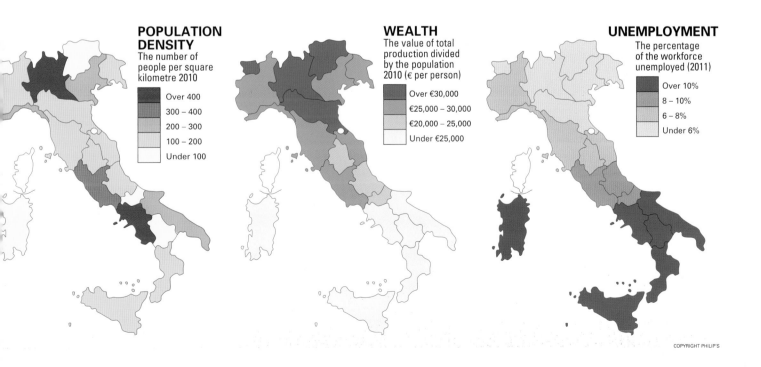

POPULATION DENSITY

The number of people per square kilometre 2010

- Over 400
- 300 – 400
- 200 – 300
- 100 – 200
- Under 100

WEALTH

The value of total production divided by the population 2010 (€ per person)

- Over €30,000
- €25,000 – 30,000
- €20,000 – 25,000
- Under €25,000

UNEMPLOYMENT

The percentage of the workforce unemployed (2011)

- Over 10%
- 8 – 10%
- 6 – 8%
- Under 6%

Asia : Relief of Land

Height of the land (metres)

over 6000
4000–6000
2000–4000
1000–2000
400–1000
200–400
0–200
below sea level

sea level

Locator map

North America · Arctic Ocean · Pacific Ocean · Oceania

Europe · Africa · Indian Ocean

Scale 1:48 000 000

COPYRIGHT PHILIP'S

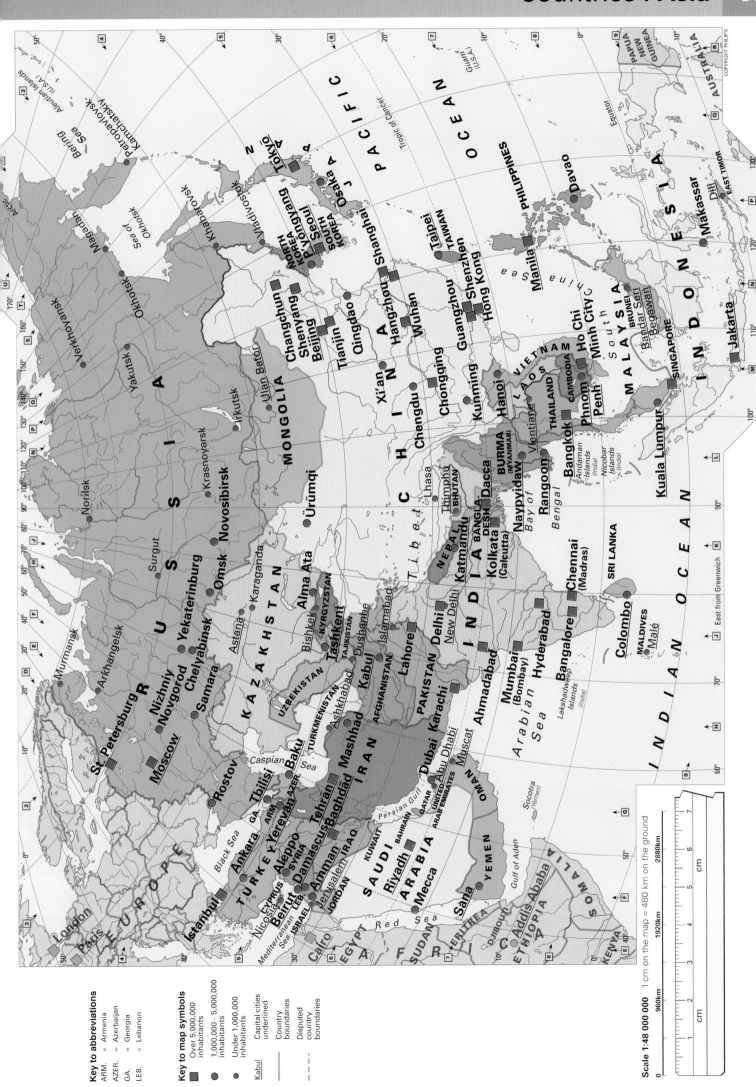

Key to abbreviations
ARM. = Armenia
AZER. = Azerbaijan
GA. = Georgia
LEB. = Lebanon

Key to map symbols
■ Over 5,000,000 inhabitants
● 1,000,000 – 5,000,000 inhabitants
• Under 1,000,000 inhabitants
Kabul Capital cities underlined
Country boundaries
Disputed country boundaries

Scale 1:48 000 000 1 cm on the map = 480 km on the ground

0   960km   1920km   2880km

cm

1 cm   2   3   4   5   6   7

Height of the land (metres)

	over 6000
	4000-6000
	2000-4000
	1000-2000
	400-1000
	200-400
	0-200
sea level	below sea level

Key to map symbols

■   Over 5,000,000 inhabitants

●   1,000,000 - 5,000,000 inhabitants

•   Under 1,000,000 inhabitants

<u>Kiev</u>   Capital cities underlined

━━━   Country boundaries

Scale 1:20 000 000   1 cm on the map = 200 km on the ground

0   500km   1000km   1500km   2000km   2500km

1   2   3   4   5   6   7   8   9   10
cm   cm   cm

Locator map

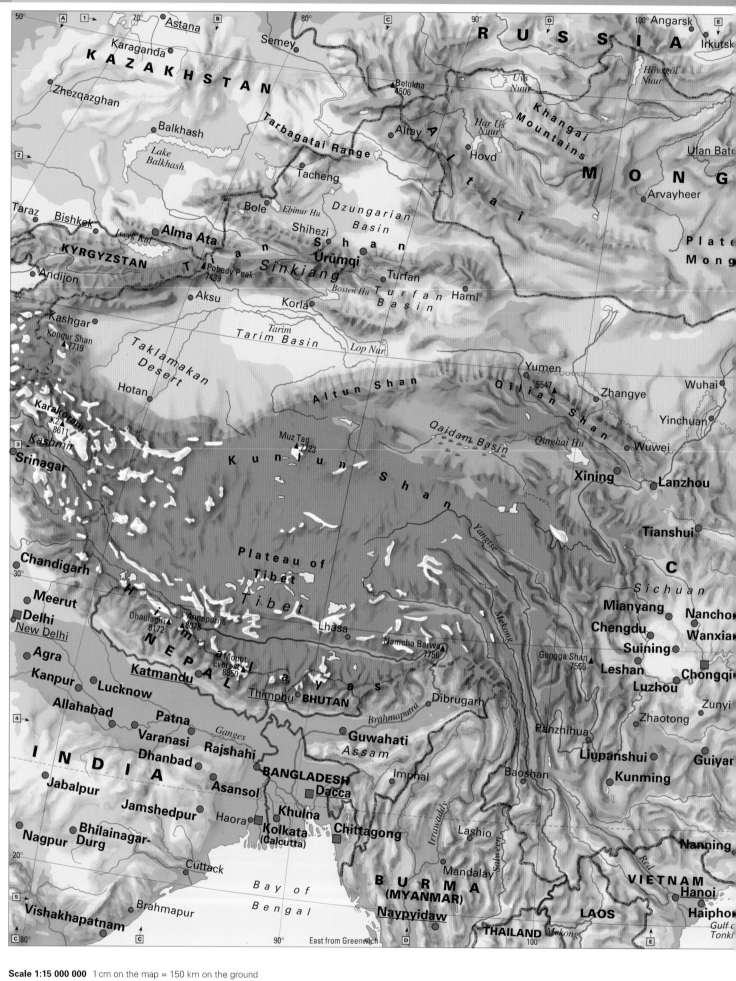

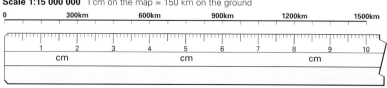

Height of the land (metres)

over 6000	
4000-6000	
2000-4000	
1000-2000	
400-1000	
200-400	
0-200	
sea level	
below sea level	

Locator map

Key to map symbols

■ Over 5,000,000 inhabitants

● 1,000,000 - 5,000,000 inhabitants

• Under 1,000,000 inhabitants

Beijing Capital cities underlined

▬▬▬ Country boundaries

▬ ▬ ▬ Disputed country boundaries

COPYRIGHT PHILIP'S

INDUSTRIAL REGIONS

- Core industrial regions
- ● Major centres for industry
- ● Centres for iron and steel, and chemicals
- ▨ Rapidly developing coastal regions
- ■ Special Economic Zones
- ▼ Special Administrative Regions
- Outer industrial regions
- Outer industrial regions with traditional heavy industry
- Remote undeveloped regions
- ← Direction of future growth
- — Important rail links

EMPLOYMENT IN INDUSTRY

Industrial workforce by province in millions

6 4 2 1 0.5

Income by province – the value of total production divided by the population in US$ 2010

- Over $10,000
- $5,000 – $10,000
- $2,500 – $5,000
- Under $2,500

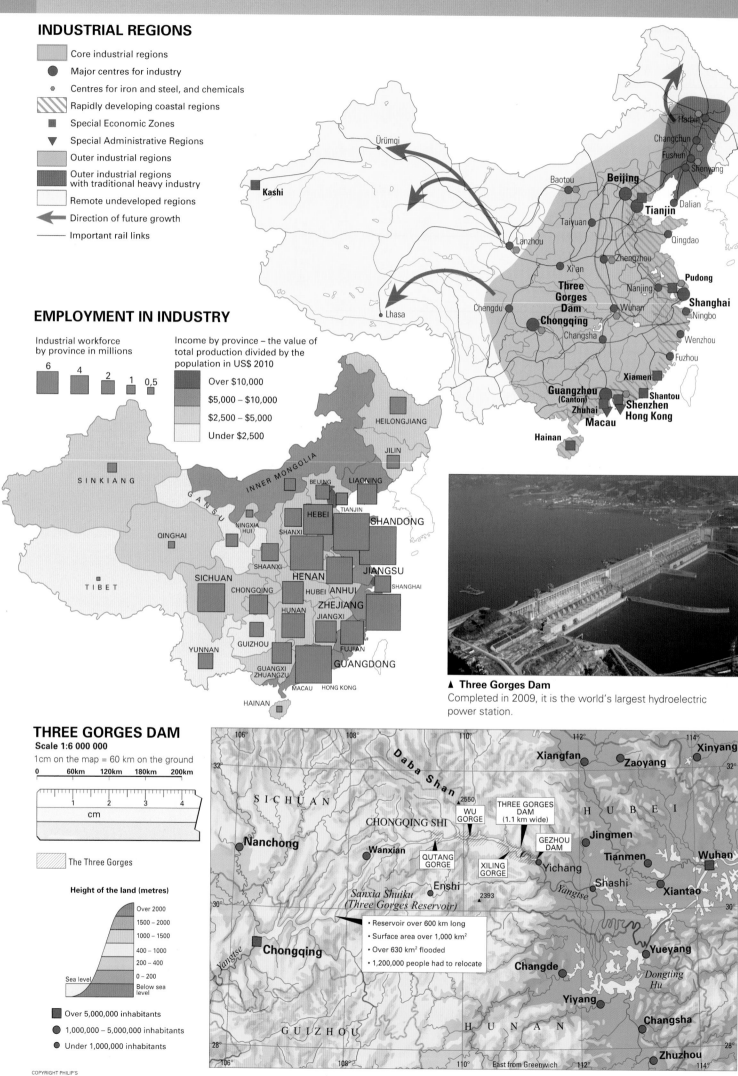

▲ **Three Gorges Dam**
Completed in 2009, it is the world's largest hydroelectric power station.

THREE GORGES DAM

Scale 1:6 000 000

1cm on the map = 60 km on the ground

0   60km   120km   180km   200km

cm

▨ The Three Gorges

Height of the land (metres)

- Over 2000
- 1500 – 2000
- 1000 – 1500
- 400 – 1000
- 200 – 400
- 0 – 200
- Sea level
- Below sea level

- ■ Over 5,000,000 inhabitants
- ● 1,000,000 – 5,000,000 inhabitants
- ● Under 1,000,000 inhabitants

Three Gorges Dam map labels:
- Reservoir over 600 km long
- Surface area over 1,000 km²
- Over 630 km² flooded
- 1,200,000 people had to relocate

THREE GORGES DAM (1.1 km wide)
WU GORGE
QUTANG GORGE
XILING GORGE
GEZHOU DAM
Sanxia Shuiku (Three Gorges Reservoir)

JAPAN EARTHQUAKE AND TSUNAMI 2011

Epicentre of earthquake 11 March 2011 (magnitude 9.0)

Observed tsunami heights

- Over 8 metres
- Over 4 metres
- Over 2 metres
- Over 1 metre

Epicentres of previous earthquakes (magnitude 7.0 or more since AD 1600)

Plate boundary

Destructive plate boundary (plates colliding)

Direction of movement

Active volcanoes

6,742 dead, or missing in Iwate Prefecture

13,818 dead, or missing in Miyagi Prefecture

1,957 dead, or missing in Fukushima Prefecture

Epicentre 11 March 2011

Fukushima Daiichi Nuclear Power Station

NORTH AMERICAN PLATE

EURASIAN PLATE

PACIFIC PLATE

PHILIPPINE PLATE

Tokyo

TOTAL JAPAN 22,589 dead, or missing

Scale 1:10 000 000
1 cm on the map = 100 km on the ground

0   100km   200km   300km   400km

1   2   3   4

cm

Height of the land (metres)

- over 4000
- 2000-4000
- 1000-2000
- 400-1000
- 200-400
- 0-200
- below sea level

Key to map symbols

- Over 5,000,000 inhabitants
- 1,000,000 – 5,000,000 inhabitants
- Under 1,000,000 inhabitants

Tōkyō Capital cities underlined

Country boundaries

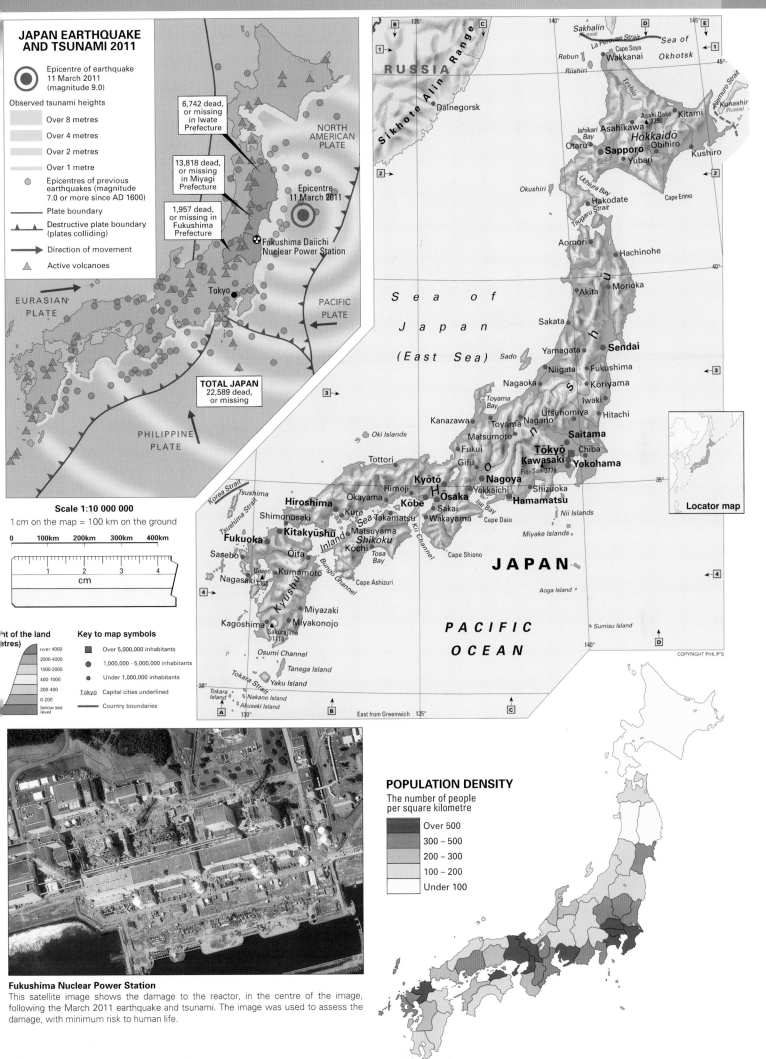

RUSSIA

Sikhote Alin Range

Dalnegorsk

Sakhalin (Russia)

La Perouse Strait

Sea of Okhotsk

Cape Soya
Wakkanai
Rebun
Riishiri
Okushiri
Ishikari Bay
Otaru
Teshio
Asahikawa
Asahi Dake 2290
Hokkaidō
Sapporo
Obihiro
Yubari
Uchiura Bay
Hakodate
Tsugaru Strait
Kitami
Kushiro
Cape Erimo
Nemuro Strait
Kunashir (Russia)

Aomori
Hachinohe
Akita
Morioka

Sea of Japan (East Sea)

Sado

Sakata
Yamagata
Sendai
Niigata
Fukushima
Nagaoka
Koriyama
Iwaki
Hitachi
Toyama Bay
Kanazawa
Toyama
Nagano
Utsunomiya
Matsumoto
Saitama
Fukui
Gifu
Tōkyō
Chiba
Kawasaki
Yokohama
Fuji-San 3776
Tottori
Kyōto
Nagoya
Yokkaichi
Shizuoka
Himeji
Ōsaka
Hamamatsu
Okayama
Kōbe
Sakai
Hiroshima
Kure
Takamatsu
Wakayama
Ise Bay
Cape Daio
Shimonoseki
Inland Sea
Matsuyama
Shikoku
Kōchi
Kii Channel
Cape Shiono
Kitakyūshū
Tosa Bay
Fukuoka
Ōita
Bungo Channel
Cape Ashizuri
Sasebo
Kumamoto
Nagasaki
Unzen 1360
Miyazaki
Miyakonojo
Kagoshima
Sakurajima 1118

Korea Strait
Tsushima
Tsushima Strait
Oki Islands

JAPAN

Nii Islands
Miyake Islands
Aoga Island
Sumisu Island

PACIFIC OCEAN

Osumi Channel
Tanega Island
Yaku Island
Tokara Strait
Tokara Island
Nakano Island
Akuseki Island

East from Greenwich

Locator map

COPYRIGHT PHILIP'S

Fukushima Nuclear Power Station
This satellite image shows the damage to the reactor, in the centre of the image, following the March 2011 earthquake and tsunami. The image was used to assess the damage, with minimum risk to human life.

POPULATION DENSITY
The number of people per square kilometre

- Over 500
- 300 – 500
- 200 – 300
- 100 – 200
- Under 100

Scale comparison map

U.K and Ireland
on same scale

Scale 1:27 500 000   1 cm on the map = 275 km on the ground

0	550km	1100km	1650km	2200km	2750km

Cross-section along latitude 30°N

IRAN   PAKISTAN   INDIA   TIBET   CHINA

Himalayas
Brahmaputra
▲ Mount Everest
8850

Persian
Gulf
Zagros
Mountains

Indus
Chenab
Sutlej

Ganges

Tibetan Plateau

Salween
Mekong
Yangtse

Yangtse

Yangtse
Yangtse

East China Sea

30°N

Height of the land (metres)

over 6000	
4000-6000	
2000-4000	
1000-2000	
400-1000	
200-400	
0-200	
sea level	below sea level

Locator map

Key to map symbols

■ Over 5,000,000 inhabitants

● 1,000,000 - 5,000,000 inhabitants

• Under 1,000,000 inhabitants

<u>Beijing</u> Capital cities underlined

━━━ Country boundaries

- - - Disputed country boundaries

Seasonal lakes

COPYRIGHT PHILIP'S

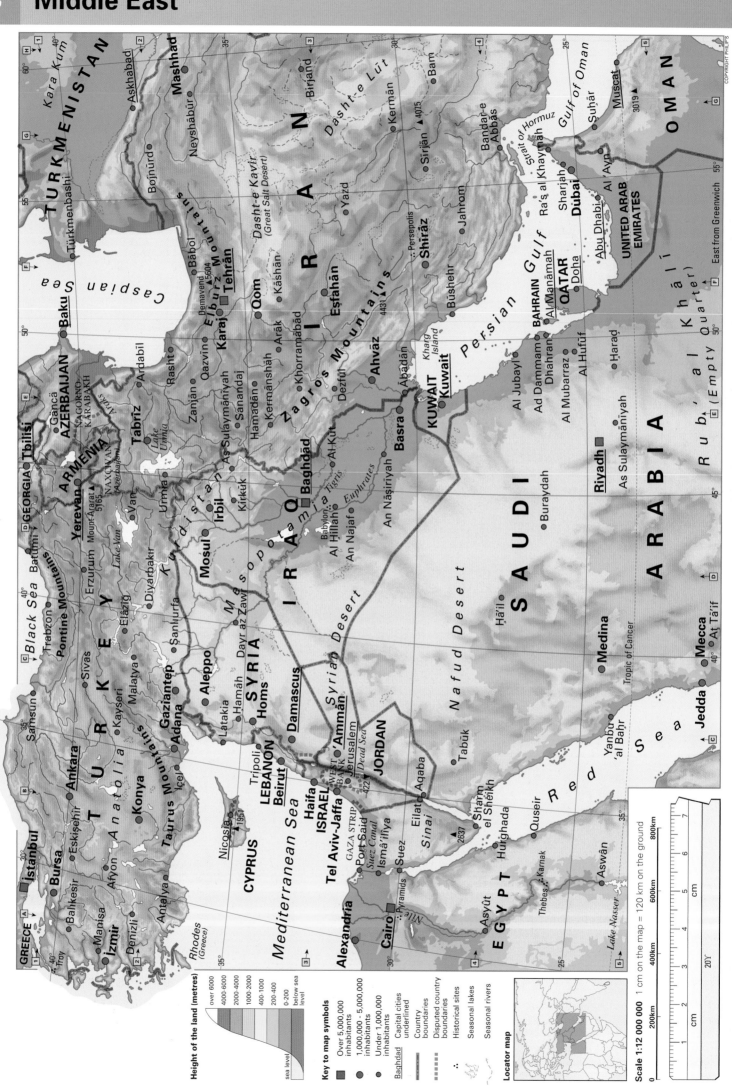

Height of the land (metres)

over 6000
4000-6000
2000-4000
1000-2000
400-1000
200-400
0-200
below sea level

sea level

Key to map symbols

- Over 5,000,000 inhabitants
- 1,000,000 - 5,000,000 inhabitants
- Under 1,000,000 inhabitants

Baghdad Capital cities underlined

Country boundaries

Disputed country boundaries

Historical sites

Seasonal lakes

Seasonal rivers

Locator map

Scale 1:12 000 000 1 cm on the map = 120 km on the ground

0   200km   400km   600km   800km

1   2   3   4   5   6   7
cm

COPYRIGHT PHILIP'S

▲ **Riyadh, Saudi Arabia**
This satellite image shows the area near the capital, Riyadh. The city is set in an arid landscape and the water supply for the city and agriculture is extracted from underground reservoirs or 'aquifers'. The green circles are fields, irrigated by centre-pivot watering systems.

WATER

- Deep fossil-water aquifer
- Dam
- Sea water desalination plant
- Freshwater pipeline
- Proposed pipeline
- Freshwater aqueduct

Average annual rainfall
- over 250 mm
- under 250 mm

Caspian Sea
Black Sea
GEORGIA
Tbilisi
ARMENIA
AZERBAIJAN
Baku
Caucasus
Elburz Mts.
Tehrān
IRAN
Ankara
TURKEY
Anatolia
Istanbul
Taurus Mts.
Karakaya Dam
Keban Dam
Batman Dam
Lake Van
Atatürk Dam
Seyhan Dam
Mosul Dam
Dicle Dam
Tigris
Euphrates
Mesopotamia
Baghdād
IRAQ
Zagros Mts.
Lake Urmia
Aras
Mediterranean Sea
CYPRUS
Beirut
LEBANON
Damascus
SYRIA
Assad Dam
Amman
JORDAN
ISRAEL
Dead Sea
Jordan
Suez Canal
Cairo
EGYPT
Nile
Aswan Dam
Lake Nasser
Toshka Lakes
Nubian Aquifer
SUDAN
Red Sea
Jedda
Mecca
Medina
Western Pipeline
Nafud Aquifer
SAUDI ARABIA
Riyadh
Riyadh Aquifer
Dhahran
Gulf Pipeline
Kuwait
KUWAIT
Persian Gulf
BAHRAIN
QATAR
Doha
U.A.E.
Abu Dhabi
Dubai
Rub' al Khali Aquifer
OMAN
Gulf of Oman
Muscat
OMAN

OIL AND GAS

- Oil
- Gas
- Oil pipeline
- Gas pipeline
- Oil pipeline under construction
- Gas pipeline under construction
- Oil refinery
- Tanker terminal

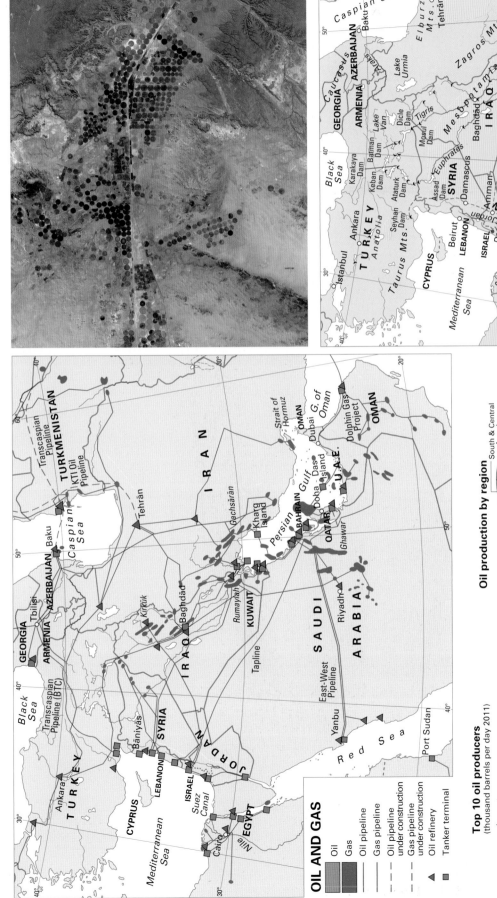

Black Sea
GEORGIA
Tbilisi
Ankara
TURKEY
CYPRUS
Mediterranean Sea
LEBANON
ISRAEL
Suez Canal
Cairo
EGYPT
Nile
JORDAN
SYRIA
Bāniyās
Transcaspian Pipeline (BTC)
Transcaspian Pipeline
ARMENIA
AZERBAIJAN
Baku
Caspian Sea
TURKMENISTAN
KT1 Oil Pipeline
Tehrān
IRAN
Kirkūk
IRAQ
Baghdād
Rumaylah
Gachsārān
Kharg Island
KUWAIT
Tapline
Riyadh
SAUDI ARABIA
East–West Pipeline
Yanbu
Red Sea
Port Sudan
BAHRAIN
Persian Gulf
QATAR
Ghawar
Doha
Das Island
U.A.E.
Dubai
Strait of Hormuz
OMAN
G. of Oman
Dolphin Gas Project
OMAN

Oil production by region

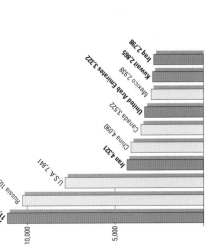

- South & Central America 9%
- Middle East 33%
- Europe & Eurasia 21%
- North America 17%
- Africa 10%
- Asia/Pacific 10%

World production (2011)
83.6 million barrels per day

Oil reserves by region

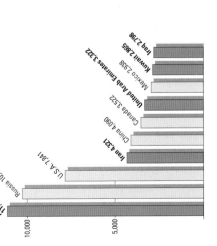

- Asia/Pacific 3%
- Middle East 48%
- South & Central America 20%
- Europe & Eurasia 8%
- Africa 8%
- North America 13%

World proved reserves (2011)
1,652.6 billion barrels

Top 10 oil producers
(thousand barrels per day 2011)

Saudi Arabia 11,161
Russia 10,280
U.S.A. 7,841
Iran 4,321
China 4,090
Canada 3,522
United Arab Emirates 3,322
Mexico 2,938
Kuwait 2,865
Iraq 2,798

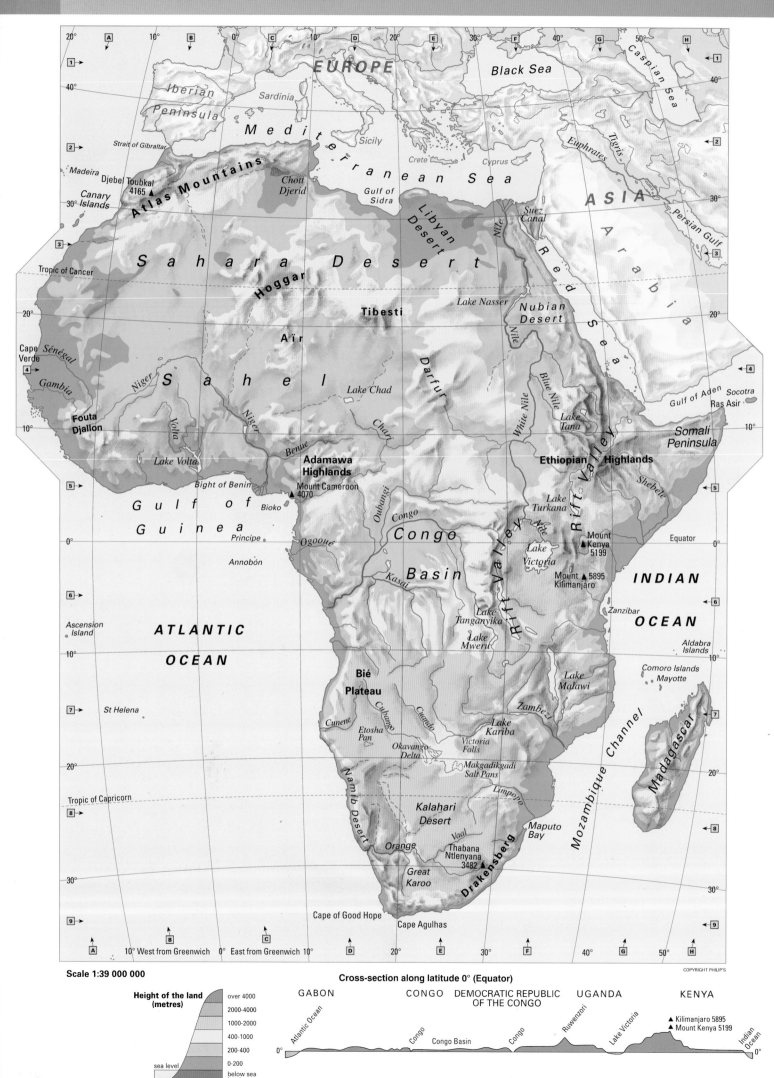

Scale 1:39 000 000

COPYRIGHT PHILIP'S

Height of the land (metres)

over 4000
2000-4000
1000-2000
400-1000
200-400
0-200
sea level
below sea level

Cross-section along latitude 0° (Equator)

GABON | CONGO | DEMOCRATIC REPUBLIC OF THE CONGO | UGANDA | KENYA

▲ Kilimanjaro 5895
▲ Mount Kenya 5199

Atlantic Ocean — Congo — Congo Basin — Congo — Ruwenzori — Lake Victoria — Indian Ocean

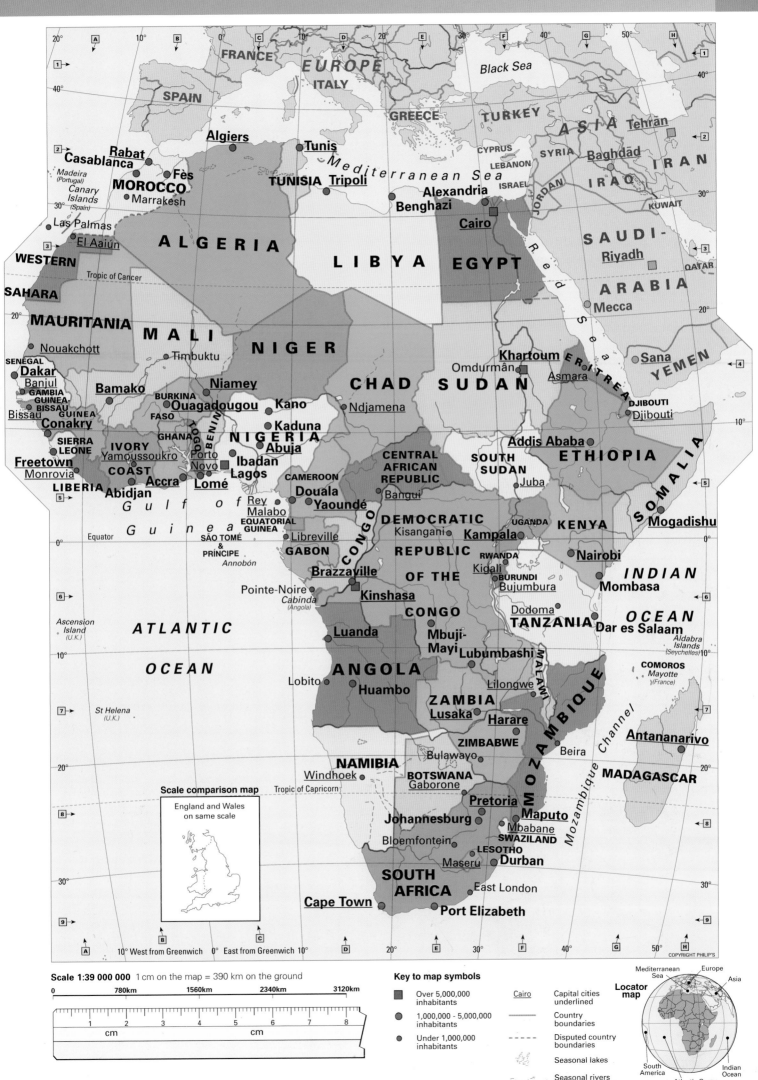

Scale 1:39 000 000 1 cm on the map = 390 km on the ground

0	780km	1560km	2340km	3120km

Key to map symbols

- ■ Over 5,000,000 inhabitants
- ● 1,000,000 – 5,000,000 inhabitants
- ● Under 1,000,000 inhabitants

Cairo — Capital cities underlined

—— Country boundaries

- - - - Disputed country boundaries

Seasonal lakes

Seasonal rivers

Locator map

Mediterranean Sea · Europe · Asia · South America · Atlantic Ocean · Indian Ocean

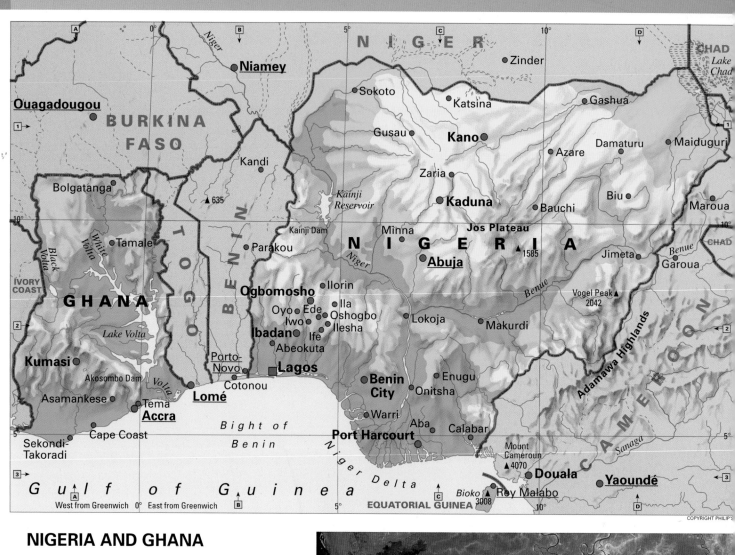

NIGERIA AND GHANA

Scale 1:10 000 000 1 cm on the map = 100 km on the ground

| 0 | 100km | 200km | 300km | 400km | 500km | 600km |

See page opposite for key to map symbols, locator map and height of the land reference panel.

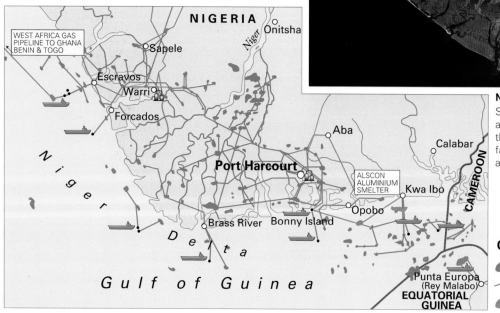

Niger Delta, Nigeria ▲

Satellite imagery helps to plan the drilling for oil and gas in the delta and to monitor the effect of the drilling on this fragile environment. This is a false colour image which shows vegetation such as mangrove swamps in dark red.

OIL AND GAS IN THE NIGER DELTA

◢ Oilfields	⌒ Gas pipelines
⌒ Oil pipelines	⛴ Tanker terminals
◣ Gasfields	⛽ Oil refineries

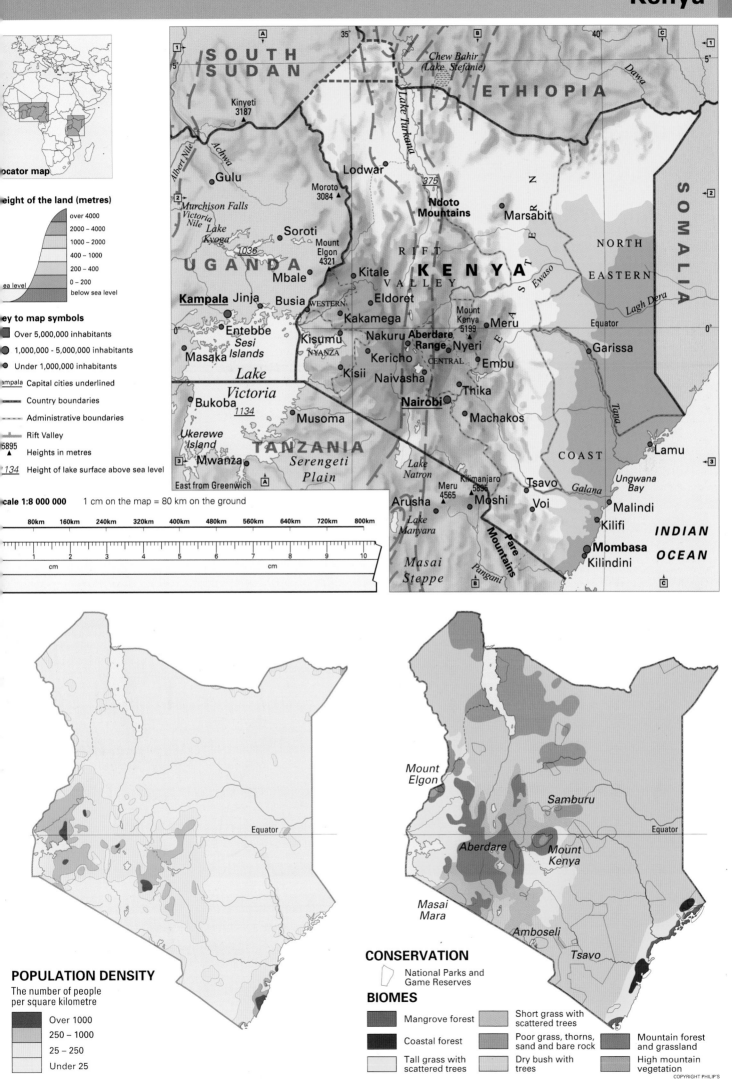

Locator map

Height of the land (metres)

	over 4000
	2000 – 4000
	1000 – 2000
	400 – 1000
	200 – 400
sea level	0 – 200
	below sea level

Key to map symbols

- ■ Over 5,000,000 inhabitants
- ● 1,000,000 – 5,000,000 inhabitants
- ● Under 1,000,000 inhabitants

Kampala Capital cities underlined

— Country boundaries

–·– Administrative boundaries

Rift Valley

▲5895 Heights in metres

_134 Height of lake surface above sea level

Scale 1:8 000 000   1 cm on the map = 80 km on the ground

80km 160km 240km 320km 400km 480km 560km 640km 720km 800km

East from Greenwich

POPULATION DENSITY

The number of people per square kilometre

	Over 1000
	250 – 1000
	25 – 250
	Under 25

CONSERVATION

⬠ National Parks and Game Reserves

BIOMES

- Mangrove forest
- Coastal forest
- Tall grass with scattered trees
- Short grass with scattered trees
- Poor grass, thorns, sand and bare rock
- Dry bush with trees
- Mountain forest and grassland
- High mountain vegetation

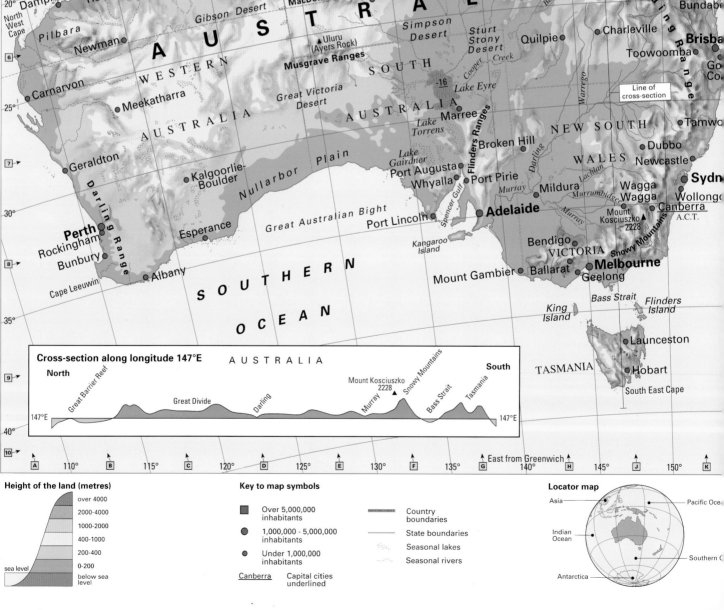

Cross-section along longitude 147°E

A U S T R A L I A

North

South

Great Barrier Reef

Great Divide

Darling

Mount Kosciuszko
2228

Murray

Snowy Mountains

Bass Strait

Tasmania

147°E

147°E

East from Greenwich

Height of the land (metres)

over 4000	
2000-4000	
1000-2000	
400-1000	
200-400	
0-200	
sea level	
below sea level	

Key to map symbols

◼ Over 5,000,000 inhabitants

● 1,000,000 - 5,000,000 inhabitants

• Under 1,000,000 inhabitants

Canberra Capital cities underlined

▦▦ Country boundaries

— State boundaries

Seasonal lakes

Seasonal rivers

Locator map

Asia

Pacific Oce

Indian Ocean

Southern

Antarctica

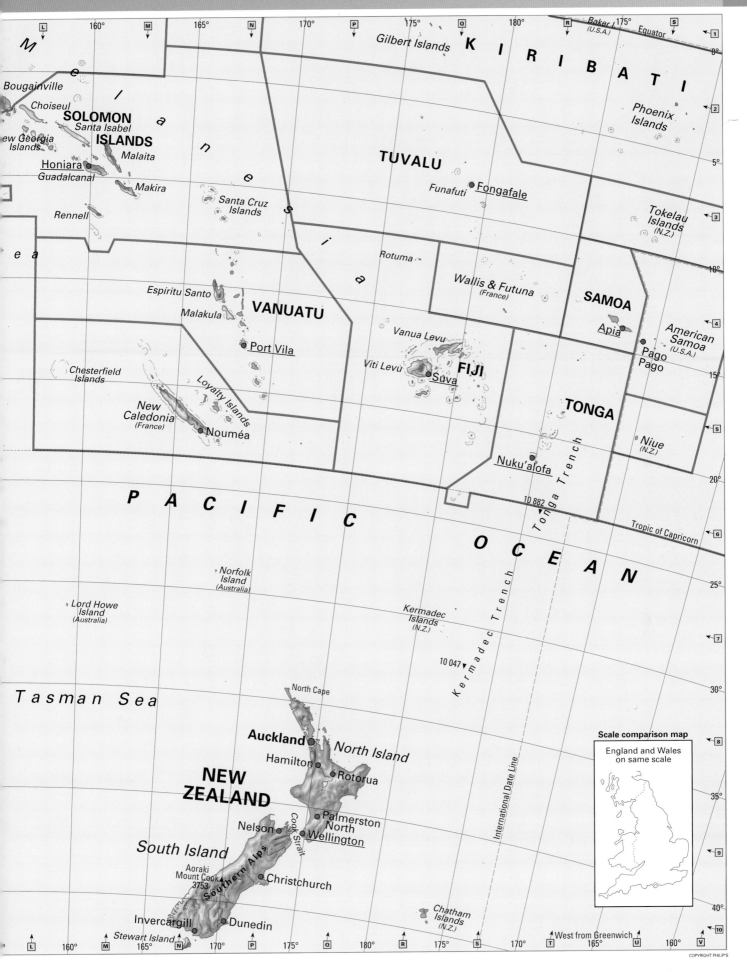

M

Gilbert Islands

K I R I B A T I

Bougainville

Choiseul
SOLOMON
Santa Isabel
ew Georgia
Islands **ISLANDS**

Malaita

Honiara
Guadalcanal

Makira

Rennell

Melanesia

Santa Cruz
Islands

Phoenix
Islands

2

TUVALU

Funafuti Fongafale

5°

Tokelau
Islands
(N.Z.)

3

ea

Rotuma

Wallis & Futuna
(France)

SAMOA

Apia

10°

Espíritu Santo

Malakula

VANUATU

Port Vila

Vanua Levu

Viti Levu

Suva **FIJI**

American
Samoa
(U.S.A.)

Pago
Pago

4

15°

Chesterfield
Islands

Loyalty Islands

New
Caledonia
(France) Nouméa

TONGA

Nuku'alofa

Niue
(N.Z.)

5

10 882

Tonga Trench

20°

P A C I F I C

Norfolk
Island
(Australia)

Tropic of Capricorn

6

Lord Howe
Island
(Australia)

O C E A N

25°

Kermadec
Islands
(N.Z.)

Kermadec Trench

7

10 047

T a s m a n   S e a

North Cape

30°

Scale comparison map

England and Wales
on same scale

8

Auckland
Hamilton
North Island
Rotorua

**NEW
ZEALAND**

Palmerston
North
Nelson Wellington

International Date Line

35°

Cook Strait

South Island

Aoraki
Mount Cook
3753
Southern Alps Christchurch

Chatham
Islands
(N.Z.)

9

40°

Invercargill Dunedin
Stewart Island

West from Greenwich

10

COPYRIGHT PHILIP'S

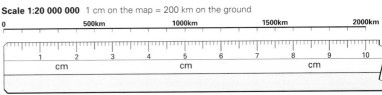

Scale 1:20 000 000 1 cm on the map = 200 km on the ground

0   500km   1000km   1500km   2000km

1   2   3   4   5   6   7   8   9   10
cm   cm   cm

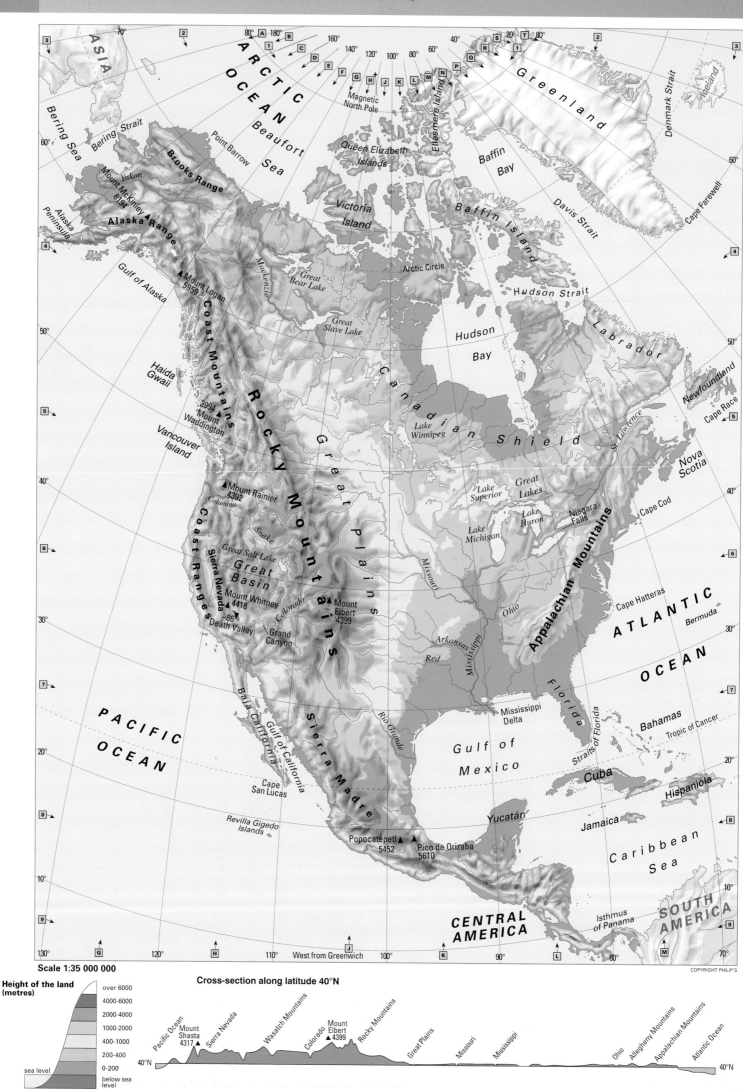

Scale 1:35 000 000

COPYRIGHT PHILIP'S

Height of the land (metres)

	over 6000
	4000–6000
	2000–4000
	1000–2000
	400–1000
	200–400
	0–200
sea level	
below sea level	

Cross-section along latitude 40°N

Pacific Ocean · Mount Shasta 4317 · Sierra Nevada · Wasatch Mountains · Colorado · Mount Elbert 4399 · Rocky Mountains · Great Plains · Missouri · Mississippi · Ohio · Allegheny Mountains · Appalachian Mountains · Atlantic Ocean

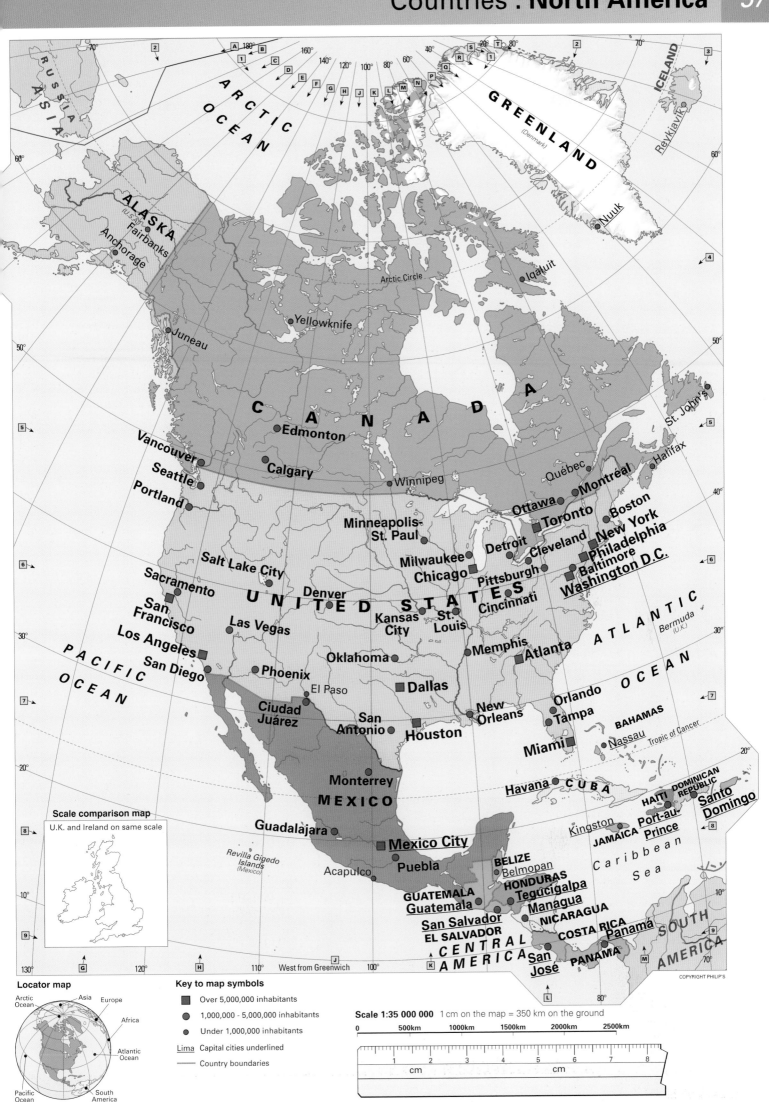

Scale comparison map
U.K. and Ireland on same scale

Locator map

Arctic Ocean
Asia
Europe
Africa
Atlantic Ocean
Pacific Ocean
South America

Key to map symbols

- ■ Over 5,000,000 inhabitants
- ● 1,000,000 - 5,000,000 inhabitants
- ● Under 1,000,000 inhabitants
- Lima Capital cities underlined
- — Country boundaries

Scale 1:35 000 000   1 cm on the map = 350 km on the ground

0   500km   1000km   1500km   2000km   2500km

COPYRIGHT PHILIP'S

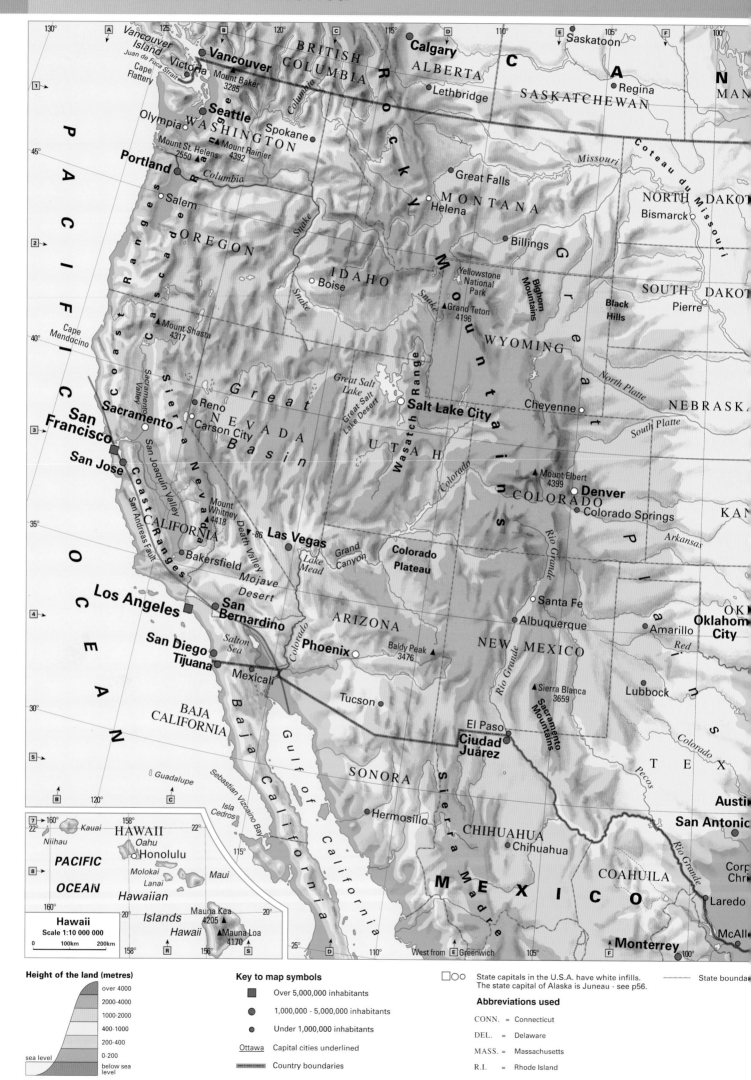

Height of the land (metres)

	over 4000
	2000-4000
	1000-2000
	400-1000
	200-400
	0-200
sea level	below sea level

Key to map symbols

■ Over 5,000,000 inhabitants

● 1,000,000 - 5,000,000 inhabitants

● Under 1,000,000 inhabitants

<u>Ottawa</u> Capital cities underlined

Country boundaries

□ □ ○ State capitals in the U.S.A. have white infills.
The state capital of Alaska is Juneau - see p56.

——— State boundar

Abbreviations used

CONN. = Connecticut

DEL. = Delaware

MASS. = Massachusetts

R.I. = Rhode Island

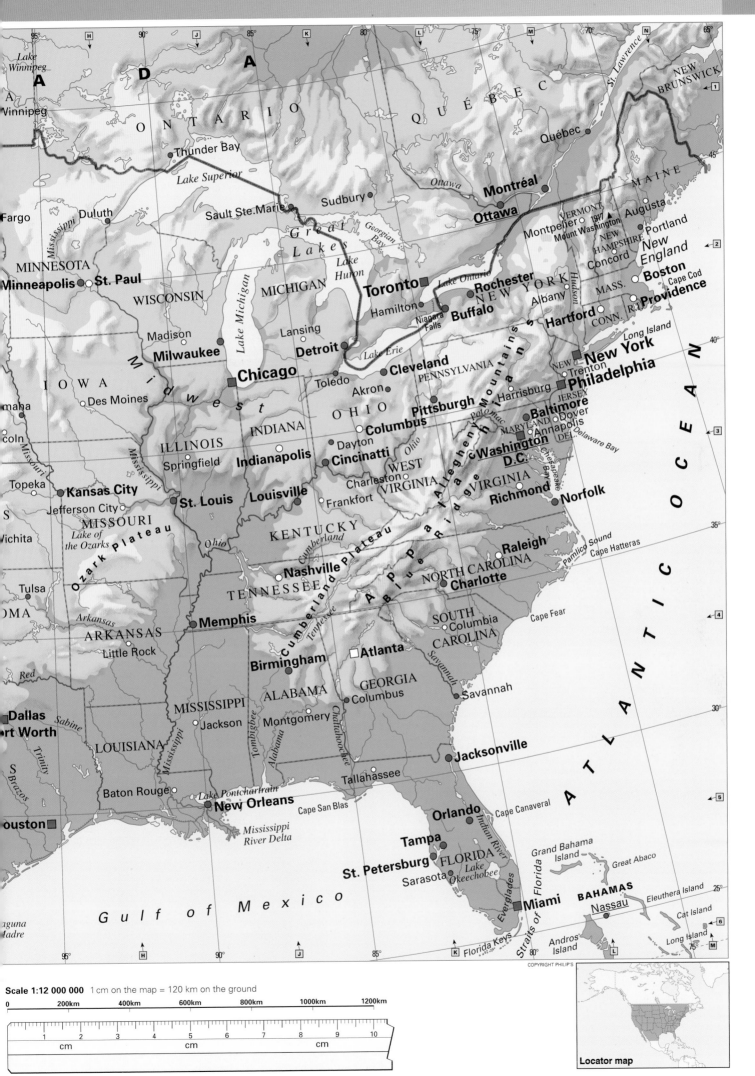

Scale 1:12 000 000   1 cm on the map = 120 km on the ground

0   200km   400km   600km   800km   1000km   1200km

1   2   3   4   5   6   7   8   9   10
cm   cm   cm

COPYRIGHT PHILIP'S

Locator map

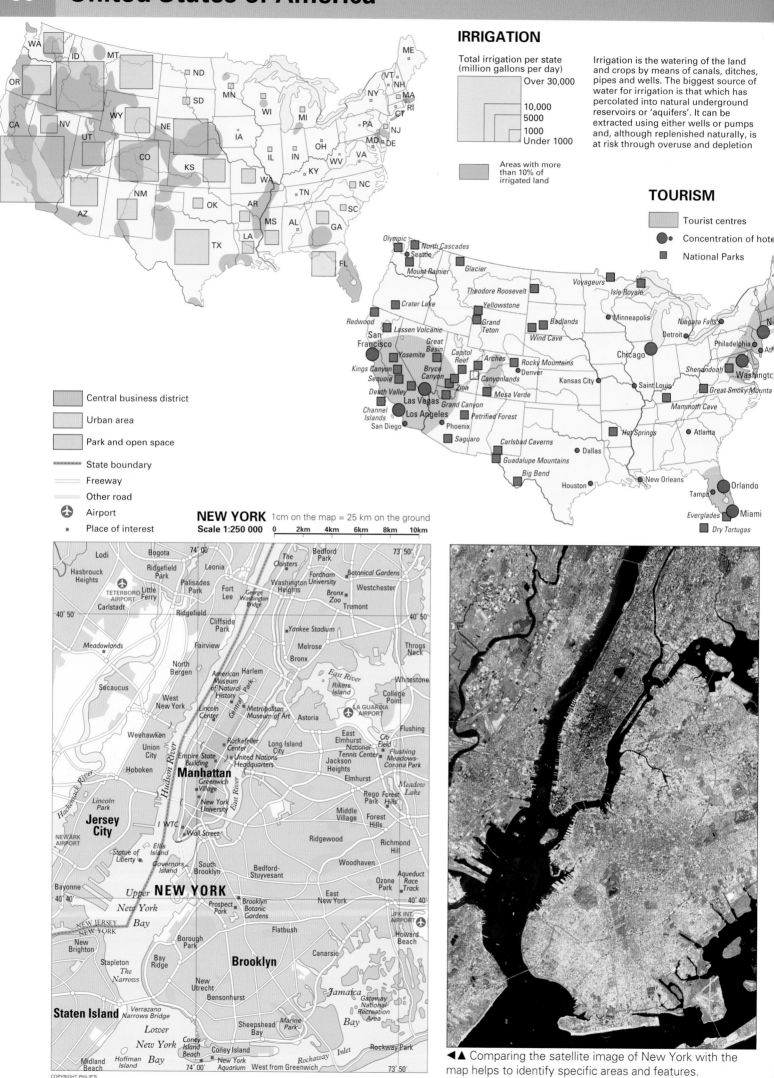

IRRIGATION

Total irrigation per state
(million gallons per day)

Over 30,000

10,000
5000
1000
Under 1000

Irrigation is the watering of the land and crops by means of canals, ditches, pipes and wells. The biggest source of water for irrigation is that which has percolated into natural underground reservoirs or 'aquifers'. It can be extracted using either wells or pumps and, although replenished naturally, is at risk through overuse and depletion

Areas with more than 10% of irrigated land

TOURISM

Tourist centres

Concentration of hot

National Parks

Central business district

Urban area

Park and open space

State boundary

Freeway

Other road

Airport

Place of interest

NEW YORK 1cm on the map = 25 km on the ground
Scale 1:250 000 0 2km 4km 6km 8km 10km

◄▲ Comparing the satellite image of New York with the map helps to identify specific areas and features.

COPYRIGHT PHILIP'S

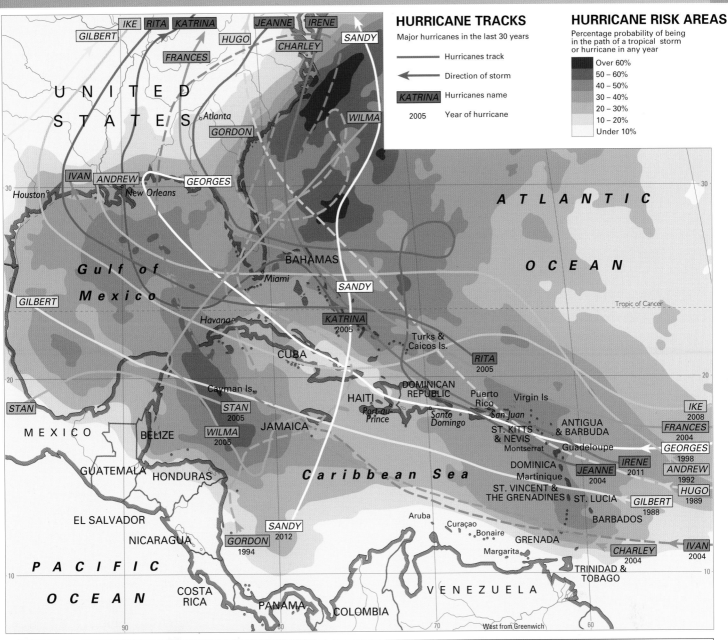

HURRICANE TRACKS

Major hurricanes in the last 30 years

⟶ Hurricanes track

⟵ Direction of storm

KATRINA   Hurricanes name

2005   Year of hurricane

HURRICANE RISK AREAS

Percentage probability of being in the path of a tropical storm or hurricane in any year

- Over 60%
- 50 – 60%
- 40 – 50%
- 30 – 40%
- 20 – 30%
- 10 – 20%
- Under 10%

▲ Hurricane Katrina hit the USA's Gulf Coast on 29 August 2005. It was the costliest and one of the five deadliest hurricanes ever to strike the United States. This satellite image shows the storm approaching the US coastline.

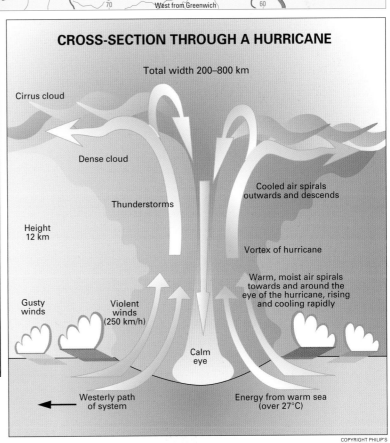

CROSS-SECTION THROUGH A HURRICANE

Total width 200–800 km

Cirrus cloud

Dense cloud

Thunderstorms

Cooled air spirals outwards and descends

Vortex of hurricane

Height 12 km

Warm, moist air spirals towards and around the eye of the hurricane, rising and cooling rapidly

Gusty winds

Violent winds (250 km/h)

Calm eye

Westerly path of system

Energy from warm sea (over 27°C)

COPYRIGHT PHILIP'S

Tijuana
Mexicali
Bataques
Phoenix
Tucson
Baja California
Colorado
Gulf of California
Nogales
El Paso
Ciudad Juárez
Río Grande do Norte
UNITED STATE
Texas
Dallas
Birmingham
Hermosillo
Sonora
Chihuahua
Conchos
Pecos
Austin
Houston
San Antonio
Mississippi
Alabama
New Orleans
Ciudad Obregón
Yaqui
Sierra Madre
3050
Nuevo Laredo
Corpus Christi
Mississippi River Delta
Los Mochis
Aguanaval
Torreón
Reynosa
Monterrey
Matamoros
Gulf of Mexico
Culiacán
La Paz
Durango
Cabo San Lucas
Mazatlán
MEXICO
Tropic of Cancer
Las Tres Marias
Río Grande de Santiago
San Luis Potosí
Aguascalientes
Tampico
Yucatán Str.
León
Guadalajara
Querétaro
Mérida
Cancún
Gulf of Campeche
Cozumel
Cabo Corrientes
Revilla Gigedo Islands
Volcán Popocatepetl
5610
Mexico
5452
Pico de Orizaba
Cuernavaca
Puebla
Veracruz
Campeche
Yucatán
Balsas
Villahermosa
Acapulco
Oaxaca
Isthmus of Tehuantepec
Chiapa
Belmopan
Belize City
BELIZE
Gulf of Honduras
Tuxtla Gutiérrez
GUATEMALA
Puerto Barrios
San Pedro Sula
HONDURAS
Gulf of Tehuantepec
4093
Guatemala
Tegucig
San Salvador
EL SALVADOR
NICARA
P A C I F I C
Managua
Lake Nicaragua
Scale comparison map
England and Wales on same scale
O C E A N
West from Greenwich

Height of the land (metres)

over 4000
2000-4000
1000-2000
400-1000
200-400
0-200
sea level
below sea level

Key to map symbols

Over 5,000,000 inhabitants

1,000,000 - 5,000,000 inhabitants

Under 1,000,000 inhabitants

Mexico Capital cities underlined

Country boundaries

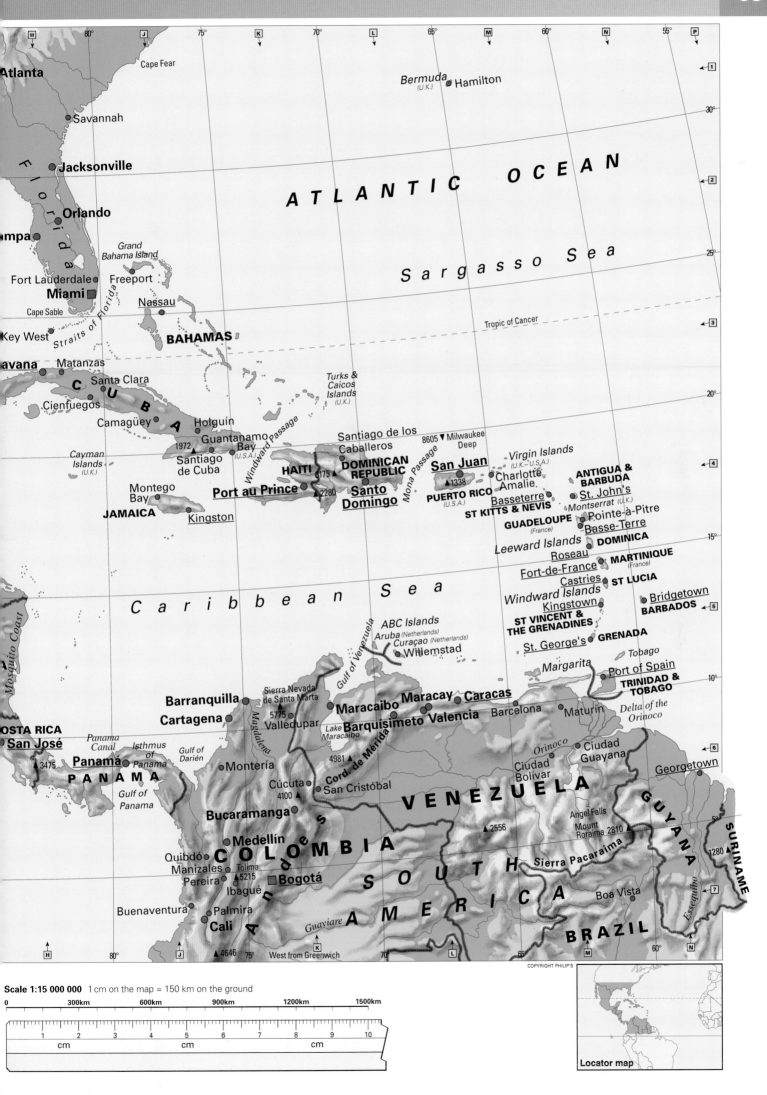

Scale 1:15 000 000 1 cm on the map = 150 km on the ground

| 0 | 300km | 600km | 900km | 1200km | 1500km |

Locator map

Height of the land (metres)

over 4000	
3000 – 4000	
2000 – 3000	
1000 – 2000	
500 – 1000	
200 – 500	
sea level 0 – 200	
below sea level	

Cross-section along latitude 20°S

CHILE   BOLIVIA   PARAGUAY   BRAZIL

▲ Ojos del Salado 6863
▲ Ancohuma & Illampu 6550

Pacific Ocean — Andes — Pilcomayo — Gran Chaco — Paraguay — Verde — Paraná — Brazilian Highlands — São Francisco — Doce — Atlantic Ocean

20°S   20°S

Scale 1:35 000 000

COPYRIGHT PHILIP'S

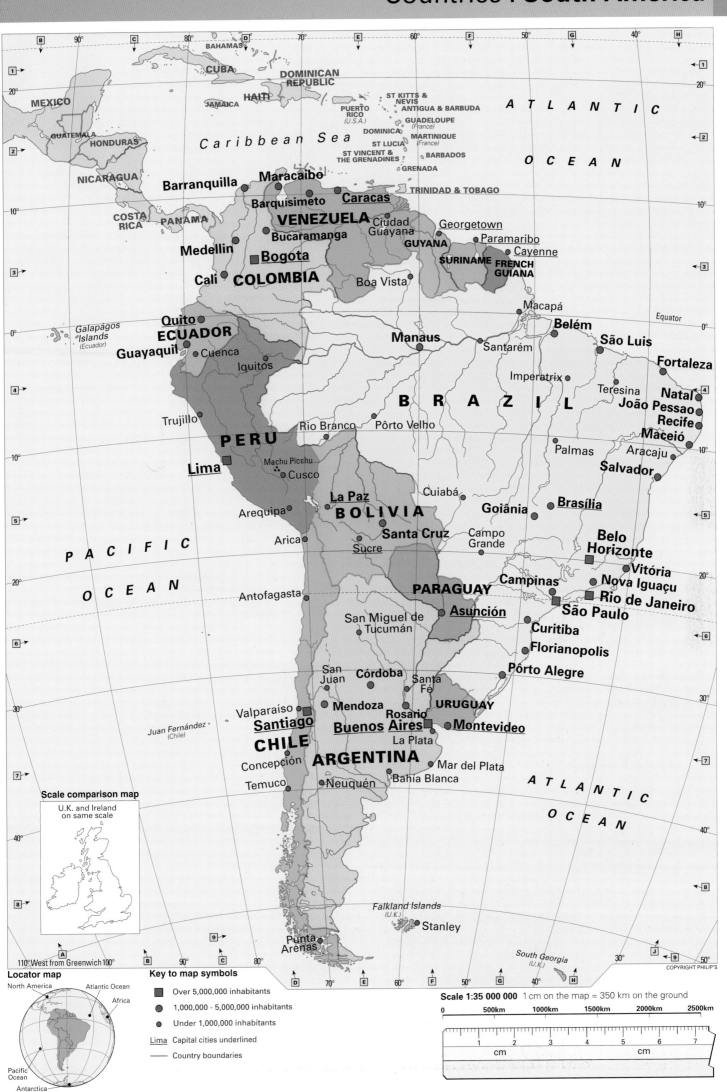

MEXICO

BAHAMAS
CUBA
DOMINICAN
REPUBLIC
HAITI
JAMAICA
PUERTO RICO (U.S.A.)

GUATEMALA
HONDURAS
NICARAGUA
COSTA RICA
PANAMA

ST KITTS & NEVIS
ANTIGUA & BARBUDA
GUADELOUPE (France)
DOMINICA
MARTINIQUE (France)
ST LUCIA
ST VINCENT & THE GRENADINES
BARBADOS
GRENADA
TRINIDAD & TOBAGO

Caribbean Sea

ATLANTIC OCEAN

Barranquilla
Maracaibo
Barquisimeto **Caracas**
VENEZUELA Ciudad Guayana
Bucaramanga
Medellin **Bogota**
Cali **COLOMBIA**
Boa Vista

Georgetown
Paramaribo
Cayenne
GUYANA SURINAME FRENCH GUIANA

Macapá

Equator

Quito **ECUADOR**
Guayaquil Cuenca
Iquitos
Trujillo
PERU
Rio Branco Pôrto Velho
Machu Picchu
Lima Cusco
La Paz
BOLIVIA
Arequipa Santa Cruz
Arica **Sucre**

Manaus
Santarém

B R A Z I L

Belém
São Luis
Fortaleza
Imperatrix
Teresina Natal
João Pessao
Recife
Maceió
Aracaju
Palmas
Salvador

Cuiabá
Goiânia **Brasília**
Campo Grande

PACIFIC OCEAN

Antofagasta

San Miguel de Tucumán

PARAGUAY
Asunción

Belo Horizonte
Vitória
Campinas Nova Iguaçu
Rio de Janeiro
São Paulo
Curitiba
Florianopolis
Pôrto Alegre

San Juan **Córdoba** Santa Fé
Valparaíso Mendoza **URUGUAY**
Santiago Rosario
CHILE Buenos Aires Montevideo
La Plata
Concepción **ARGENTINA** Mar del Plata
Temuco Bahia Blanca
Neuquén

ATLANTIC OCEAN

Juan Fernández (Chile)

Falkland Islands (U.K.)
Stanley

Punta Arenas

South Georgia (U.K.)

110° West from Greenwich 100°

COPYRIGHT PHILIP'S

Scale comparison map
U.K. and Ireland on same scale

Locator map
North America
Atlantic Ocean
Africa
Pacific Ocean
Antarctica

Key to map symbols

■ Over 5,000,000 inhabitants
● 1,000,000 - 5,000,000 inhabitants
• Under 1,000,000 inhabitants
Lima Capital cities underlined
— Country boundaries

Scale 1:35 000 000 1 cm on the map = 350 km on the ground

0   500km 1000km 1500km 2000km 2500km

1   2   3   4   5   6   7
cm   cm

VENEZUELA

Orinoco

GUYANA

SURINAME

FRENCH GUIANA

Boa Vista

Guiana Highlands

AMAPÁ

COLOMBIA

Pico de Neblina 2994

RORAIMA

Macapá

ATLANTIC OCEAN

Locator map

Equator

Uaupés

Negro

Bragança

Belém

São Luís

Parnaíba

Japurá

Solimões

Santarém

Amazon

Bacabal

Fortaleza

Içá

Putumayo

Manaus

MARANHÃO

Teresina

Mossoró

RIO GRAN DO NORT

Juruá

Purus

Madeira

A M A Z O N A S

Selvas

P A R Á

Marabá

Imperatriz

CEARÁ

Natal

Jo

Pes

Juàzeiro do Norte

PARAÍBA

Campina Grande

Rec

PIAUÍ

PERNAMBUCO

Tapajós

Aripuanã

Teles Pires

Xingu

Araguaia

Tocantins

Sobradinho Reservoir

São Francisco

Juàzeiro

Maceió

ALAGOAS

A C R E

Rio Branco

Pôrto Velho

B R A Z I L

Aracaju

SERGIPE

10°

R O N D Ô N I A

Palmas

TOCANTINS

B A H Í A

Feira de Santana

Salvador

PERU

Mamoré

Guaporé

M A T O   G R O S S O

Vitória da Conquista

Itabuna

BOLIVIA

15°

Cuiabá

Anápolis

Brasília

Montes Claros

Teófilo Otoni

15°

Goiânia

GOIÁS

Brazilian Highlands

ESPÍRITO SANTO

Scale 1:21 000 000 1 cm on the map = 210 km on the ground

MATO GROSSO DO SUL

Uberlândia

MINAS GERAIS

Belo Horizonte

Pico da Bandeira 2890

Vitória

20°

0 210km 420km 630km 840km 1050km 1260km

Campo Grande

Araçatuba

SÃO PAULO

Ribeirão Prêto

Juiz de Fora

Campos

cm

Bauru

Londrina

Paraná

Campinas

Nova Iguaçu

Rio de Janeiro

Tropic of Capricorn

São Paulo

Santos

Height of the land (metres)

Key to map symbols

PARANÁ

Ponta Grossa

over 4000

Over 5,000,000 inhabitants

Foz do Iguaçu

Curitiba

ATLANTIC

2000 – 4000

1,000,000 – 5,000,000 inhabitants

Joinville

OCEAN

1000 – 2000

SANTA CATARINA

Florianópolis

400 – 1000

Under 1,000,000 inhabitants

Iguaçu

200 – 400

Brasília Capital cities underlined

ARGENTINA

sea level

0 – 200

below sea level

Country boundaries

State boundaries

RIO GRANDE DO SUL

Caxias do Sul

PARAGUAY

URUGUAY

Uruguaiana

Pôrto Alegre

30°

Lagoa dos Patos

45°

West from Greenwich

30°

Pelotas

55°

50°

WEALTH

The value of total production divided by the population in US$ 2010

Over $10,000

$7,500 – 10,000

$5,000 – 7,500

Under $5,000

COPYRIGHT PHILIP'S

POPULATION DENSITY

The number of people per square kilometre

Over 100

50 – 100

10 – 50

Under 10

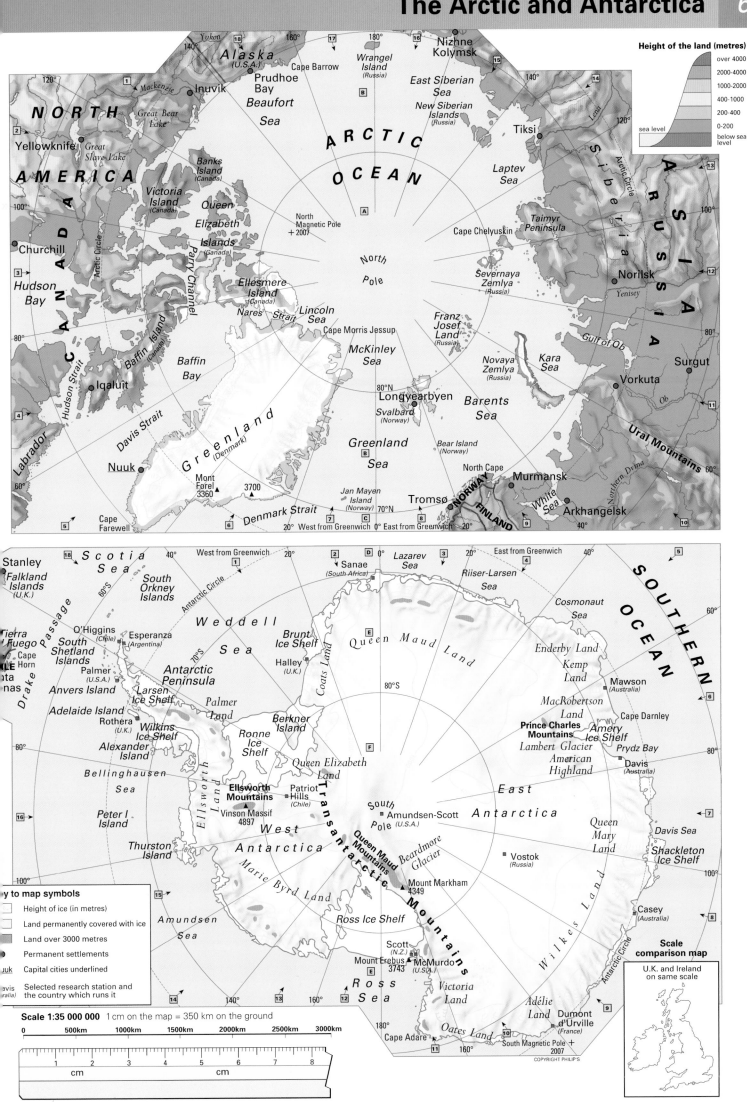

Height of the land (metres)

- over 4000
- 2000–4000
- 1000–2000
- 400–1000
- 200–400
- sea level 0–200
- below sea level

The Arctic (North)

Yukon · Alaska (U.S.A.) · Cape Barrow · Wrangel Island (Russia) · Nizhne Kolymsk · East Siberian Sea · New Siberian Islands (Russia) · Laptev Sea · Tiksi · Lena · Siberia · RUSSIA

Mackenzie · Inuvik · Prudhoe Bay · Beaufort Sea · Cape Chelyuskin · Taimyr Peninsula · Arctic Circle

NORTH · Great Bear Lake · ARCTIC OCEAN

AMERICA · Yellowknife · Great Slave Lake · Banks Island (Canada) · Queen Elizabeth Islands (Canada) · North Magnetic Pole +2007 · North Pole · Severnaya Zemlya (Russia) · Norilsk · Yenisey

CANADA · Churchill · Arctic Circle · Ellesmere Island (Canada) · Franz Josef Land (Russia) · Novaya Zemlya (Russia) · Kara Sea · Gulf of Ob · Surgut

Hudson Bay · Nares Strait · Lincoln Sea · Cape Morris Jessup · McKinley Sea · Vorkuta · Ob

Baffin Island (Canada) · Baffin Bay · 80°N · Longyearbyen · Barents Sea

Iqaluit · Svalbard (Norway) · Ural Mountains

Labrador · Hudson Strait · Davis Strait · Greenland (Denmark) · Bear Island (Norway) · North Cape · Murmansk · Northern Dvina · 60°

Nuuk · Greenland Sea · Jan Mayen Island (Norway) · NORWAY · FINLAND · White Sea · Arkhangelsk

Mont Forel 3360 · 3700 · 70°N · Tromsø

Cape Farewell · Denmark Strait · 20° West from Greenwich · 0° East from Greenwich · 20° · 40°

Antarctica (South)

Stanley · Falkland Islands (U.K.) · Scotia Sea · 40° West from Greenwich · 20° · Sanae (South Africa) · Lazarev Sea · Riiser-Larsen Sea · East from Greenwich · 40° · SOUTHERN OCEAN

South Orkney Islands · Antarctic Circle · 60°S · Cosmonaut Sea

Tierra del Fuego · Drake Passage · O'Higgins (Chile) · Esperanza (Argentina) · South Shetland Islands · Weddell Sea · Brunt Ice Shelf · Queen Maud Land · Enderby Land · Kemp Land

Cape Horn · Palmer (U.S.A.) · Antarctic Peninsula · 70°S · Halley (U.K.) · Coats Land · Mawson (Australia)

Anvers Island · Larsen Ice Shelf · MacRobertson Land · Cape Darnley

Adelaide Island · Palmer Land · Berkner Island · 80°S · Prince Charles Mountains · Amery Ice Shelf · Prydz Bay

Rothera (U.K.) · Wilkins Ice Shelf · Ronne Ice Shelf · Lambert Glacier · American Highland · Davis (Australia)

Alexander Island · Ellsworth Land · Queen Elizabeth Land · East Antarctica

Bellingshausen Sea · Ellsworth Mountains · Patriot Hills (Chile) · South Pole · Amundsen-Scott (U.S.A.) · Queen Mary Land · Davis Sea

Peter I Island · Vinson Massif 4897 · West Antarctica · Queen Maud Mountains · Beardmore Glacier · Vostok (Russia) · Shackleton Ice Shelf

Thurston Island · Marie Byrd Land · Transantarctic Mountains · Mount Markham 4349 · Wilkes Land · Casey (Australia)

Amundsen Sea · Ross Ice Shelf · Scott (N.Z.) · Mount Erebus 3743 · McMurdo (U.S.A.) · Victoria Land · Adélie Land · Dumont d'Urville (France)

Ross Sea · Cape Adare · South Magnetic Pole +2007 · Oates Land

COPYRIGHT PHILIP'S

Key to map symbols

- Height of ice (in metres)
- Land permanently covered with ice
- Land over 3000 metres
- Permanent settlements
- _Nuuk_ Capital cities underlined
- _Davis (Australia)_ Selected research station and the country which runs it

Scale 1:35 000 000   1 cm on the map = 350 km on the ground

0	500km	1000km	1500km	2000km	2500km	3000km

Scale comparison map

U.K. and Ireland on same scale

CONTINENT	AREA '000 kilometres	COLDEST PLACE degrees Celsius		HOTTEST PLACE degrees Celsius		WETTEST PLACE average annual rainfall, mm		DRIEST PLACE average annual rainfall,
Asia	44,500	Oymyakon, Russia –70°C	1	Tirat Zevi, Israel 54°C	8	Mawsynram, India 11,870	15	Aden, Yemen 46
Africa	30,302	Ifrane, Morocco –24°C	2	Al Aziziyah, Libya 58°C	9	Debundscha, Cameroon 10,290	16	Wadi Haifa, Sudan 3
North America	24,241	Snag, Yukon –63°C	3	Death Valley, California 57°C	10	Henderson Lake, Canada 6,500	17	Bataques, Mexico 30
South America	17,793	Sarmiento, Argentina –33°C	4	Rivadavia, Argentina 49°C	11	Quibdó, Colombia 8,990	18	Quillagua, Chile 0.6
Antarctica	14,000	Vostok –89°C	5	Vanda Station 15°C	12			
Europe	9,957	Ust Shchugor, Russia –55°C	6	Seville, Spain 50°C	13	Crkvice, Montenegro 4,650	19	Astrakhan, Russia 160
Oceania	8,557	Charlotte Pass, Australia –22°C	7	Oodnadatta, Australia 51°C	14	Tully, Australia 4,550	20	Mulka, Australia 100

Equatorial Scale 1:95 000 000
1 cm on the map = 950 km on the ground

Height of the land (metres)

- over 6000
- 4000 – 6000
- 2000 – 4000
- 1000 – 2000
- 200 – 1000
- 0 – 200

below sea level

COPYRIGHT PHILIP'S

LARGEST SEAS '000 square kilometres		LARGEST LAKES '000 square kilometres		LONGEST RIVERS kilometres		LARGEST ISLANDS '000 square kilometres		HIGHEST PEAKS metres		DEEPEST TRENCHES metres	
...ic Ocean 155,557	27	Caspian Sea 371	37	Nile 6,695	47	Greenland 2,176	57	Himalayas: Mount Everest 8,850	67	Mariana Trench 11,022	77
...tic Ocean 76,762	28	Lake Superior 82	38	Amazon 6,450	48	New Guinea 821	58	Karakoram: K2 8,611	68	Tonga Trench 10,822	78
...n Ocean 68,556	29	Lake Victoria 68	39	Yangtse 6,380	49	Borneo 744	59	Pamirs: Ismail Samani Peak 7,495	69	Japan Trench 10,554	79
...hern Ocean 20,237	30	Lake Huron 60	40	Mississippi-Missouri 5,971	50	Madagascar 587	60	Tian Shan: Pobedy Peak 7,439	70	Kuril Trench 10,542	80
...c Ocean 14,351	31	Lake Michigan 58	41	Yenisey-Angara 5,550	51	Baffin Island 508	61	Andes: Aconcagua 6,962	71	Mindanao Trench 10,497	81
...terranean Sea 2,966	32	Lake Tanganyika 33	42	Hwang-Ho 5,464	52	Sumatra 474	62	Rocky Mountains: Mount McKinley 6,194	72	Kermadec Trench 10,047	82
...h China Sea 2,318	33	Great Bear Lake 32	43	Ob-Irtysh 5,410	53	Honshu 231	63	East Africa: Kilimanjaro 5,895	73	Bougainville Trench 9,140	83
...ng Sea 2,274	34	Lake Baikal 31	44	Congo 4,670	54	Great Britain 230	64	Caucasus: Elbrus 5,642	74	Milwaukee Deep 8,605	84
...bean Sea 1,942	35	Lake Malawi 30	45	Mekong 4,500	55	Victoria Island 212	65	Antarctica: Vinson Massif 4,897	75	South Sandwich Trench 7,235	85
...of Mexico 1,813	36	Great Slave Lake 29	46	Amur 4,442	56	Ellesmere Island 197	66	Alps: Mont Blanc 4,808	76	Aleutian Trench 7,822	86

ALB. = ALBANIA
B.-H. = BOSNIA-HERZEGOVINA
BELG. = BELGIUM
CR. = CROATIA
CZECH. = CZECH REPUBLIC
EST. = ESTONIA
HUNG. = HUNGARY
K. = KOSOVO
LAT. = LATVIA
LEB. = LEBANON
LITH. = LITHUANIA
LUX. = LUXEMBOURG

COUNTRY	'000 people	COUNTRY	'000 people	COUNTRY	'000 people	COUNTRY	'000 people	COUNTRY	'000 peop
China	1,343,240	Mexico	114,975	France	65,631	Kenya	43,013	Nepal	29,8
India	1,205,074	Philippines	103,775	United Kingdom	63,047	Argentina	42,192	Peru	29,5
USA	313,847	Vietnam	91,519	Italy	61,261	Poland	38,415	Malaysia	29,1
Indonesia	248,645	Ethiopia	91,196	Burma	54,585	Algeria	37,367	Uzbekistan	28,3
Brazil	199,321	Egypt	83,688	South Africa	50,590	Canada	34,300	Venezuela	28,0
Pakistan	190,291	Germany	81,306	South Korea	48,861	Sudan	34,207	Saudi Arabia	26,5
Nigeria	170,124	Turkey	79,749	Spain	47,043	Uganda	33,641	Yemen	24,7
Bangladesh	161,084	Iran	78,869	Tanzania	46,913	Morocco	32,310	Ghana	24,6
Russia	142,518	Congo (Dem. Rep.)	73,599	Colombia	45,239	Iraq	31,129	North Korea	24,5
Japan	127,368	Thailand	67,091	Ukraine	44,854	Afghanistan	30,420	Mozambique	23,5

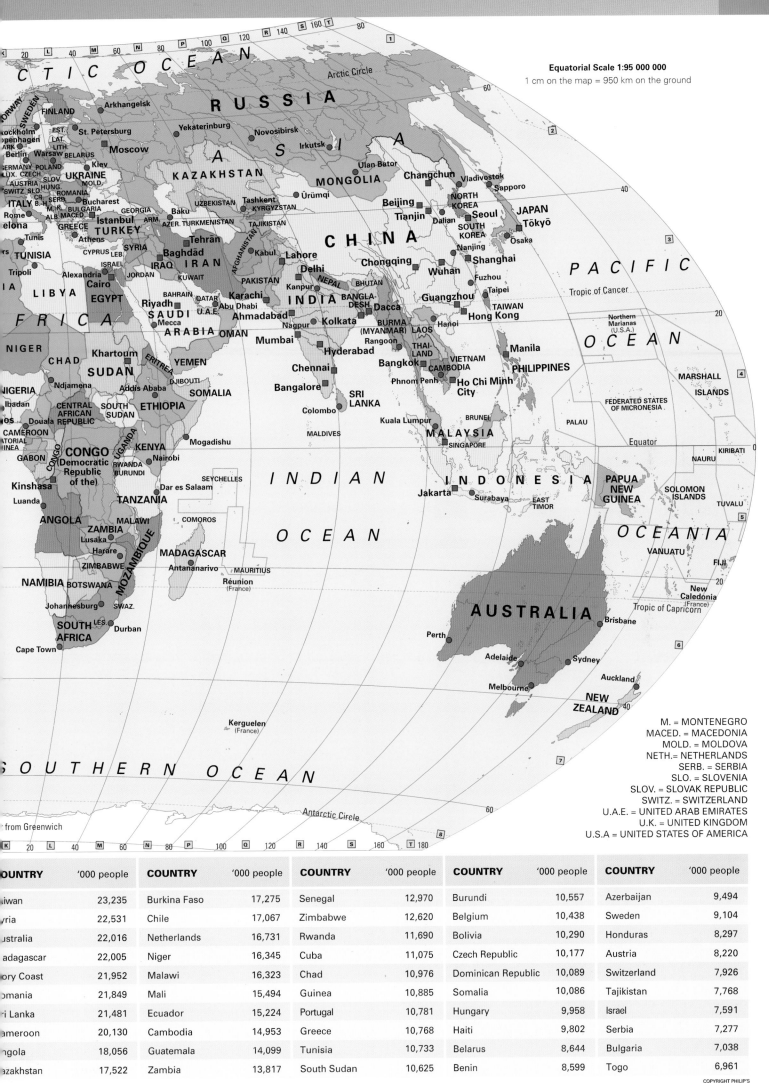

Equatorial Scale 1:95 000 000
1 cm on the map = 950 km on the ground

M. = MONTENEGRO
MACED. = MACEDONIA
MOLD. = MOLDOVA
NETH.= NETHERLANDS
SERB. = SERBIA
SLO. = SLOVENIA
SLOV. = SLOVAK REPUBLIC
SWITZ. = SWITZERLAND
U.A.E. = UNITED ARAB EMIRATES
U.K. = UNITED KINGDOM
U.S.A = UNITED STATES OF AMERICA

COUNTRY	'000 people	COUNTRY	'000 people	COUNTRY	'000 people	COUNTRY	'000 people	COUNTRY	'000 people
iwan	23,235	Burkina Faso	17,275	Senegal	12,970	Burundi	10,557	Azerbaijan	9,494
yria	22,531	Chile	17,067	Zimbabwe	12,620	Belgium	10,438	Sweden	9,104
ustralia	22,016	Netherlands	16,731	Rwanda	11,690	Bolivia	10,290	Honduras	8,297
adagascar	22,005	Niger	16,345	Cuba	11,075	Czech Republic	10,177	Austria	8,220
ory Coast	21,952	Malawi	16,323	Chad	10,976	Dominican Republic	10,089	Switzerland	7,926
omania	21,849	Mali	15,494	Guinea	10,885	Somalia	10,086	Tajikistan	7,768
ri Lanka	21,481	Ecuador	15,224	Portugal	10,781	Hungary	9,958	Israel	7,591
ameroon	20,130	Cambodia	14,953	Greece	10,768	Haiti	9,802	Serbia	7,277
ngola	18,056	Guatemala	14,099	Tunisia	10,733	Belarus	8,644	Bulgaria	7,038
azakhstan	17,522	Zambia	13,817	South Sudan	10,625	Benin	8,599	Togo	6,961

CLIMATE REGIONS

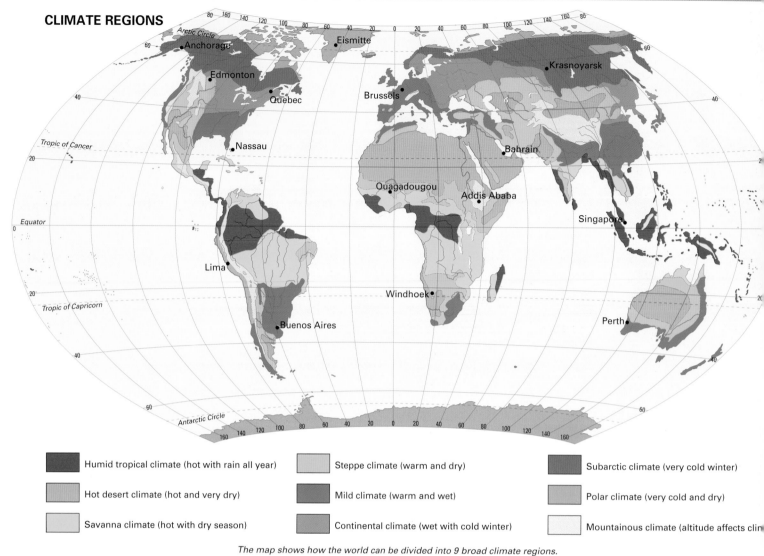

	Humid tropical climate (hot with rain all year)		Steppe climate (warm and dry)		Subarctic climate (very cold winter)
	Hot desert climate (hot and very dry)		Mild climate (warm and wet)		Polar climate (very cold and dry)
	Savanna climate (hot with dry season)		Continental climate (wet with cold winter)		Mountainous climate (altitude affects clin

The map shows how the world can be divided into 9 broad climate regions.

CLIMATE GRAPHS

The graphs below give examples of places within each climate region, showing how temperature and rainfall vary from month to month.

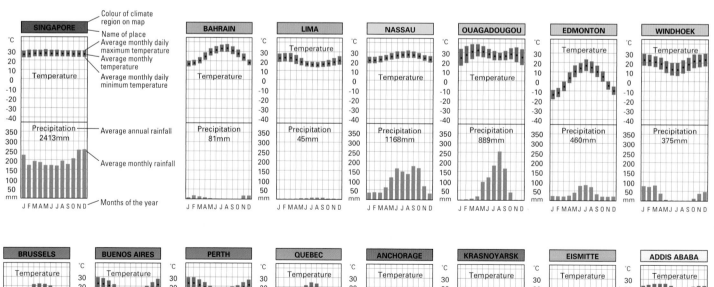

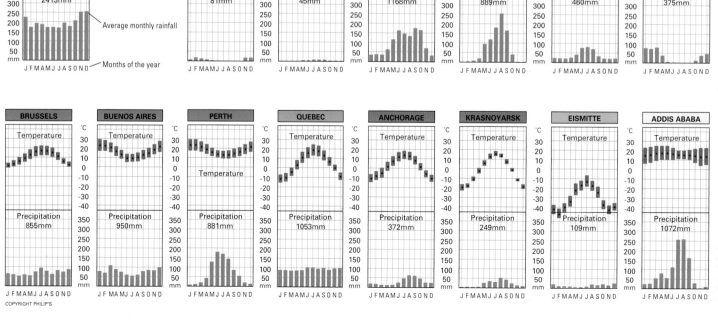

HUMID TROPICAL CLIMATE

HOT DESERT CLIMATE

SAVANNA

MILD CLIMATE

POLAR CLIMATE

MOUNTAINOUS CLIMATE

ANNUAL RAINFALL

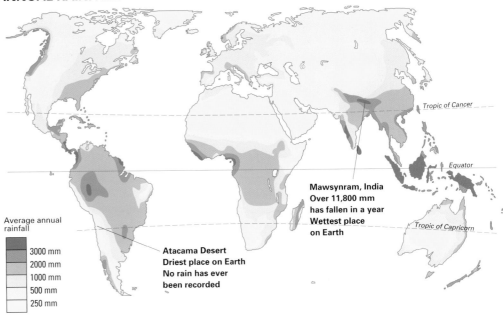

Tropic of Cancer

Equator

Mawsynram, India
Over 11,800 mm
has fallen in a year
Wettest place
on Earth

Tropic of Capricorn

Average annual
rainfall

- 3000 mm
- 2000 mm
- 1000 mm
- 500 mm
- 250 mm

Atacama Desert
Driest place on Earth
No rain has ever
been recorded

JANUARY TEMPERATURE

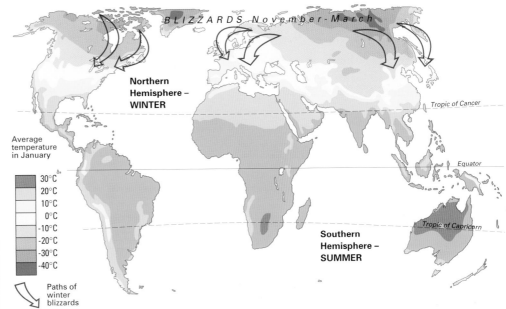

BLIZZARDS November-March

Northern
Hemisphere –
WINTER

Tropic of Cancer

Average
temperature
in January

- 30°C
- 20°C
- 10°C
- 0°C
- -10°C
- -20°C
- -30°C
- -40°C

Equator

Southern
Hemisphere –
SUMMER

Tropic of Capricorn

Paths of
winter
blizzards

JULY TEMPERATURE

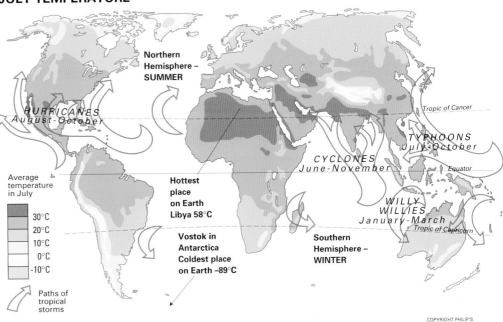

Northern
Hemisphere –
SUMMER

*HURRICANES
August-October*

Tropic of Cancer

*TYPHOONS
July-October*

*CYCLONES
June-November*

Equator

Average
temperature
in July

- 30°C
- 20°C
- 10°C
- 0°C
- -10°C

Hottest
place
on Earth
Libya 58°C

Vostok in
Antarctica
Coldest place
on Earth –89°C

Southern
Hemisphere –
WINTER

*WILLY
WILLIES
January-March*

Tropic of Capricorn

Paths of
tropical
storms

COPYRIGHT PHILIP'S

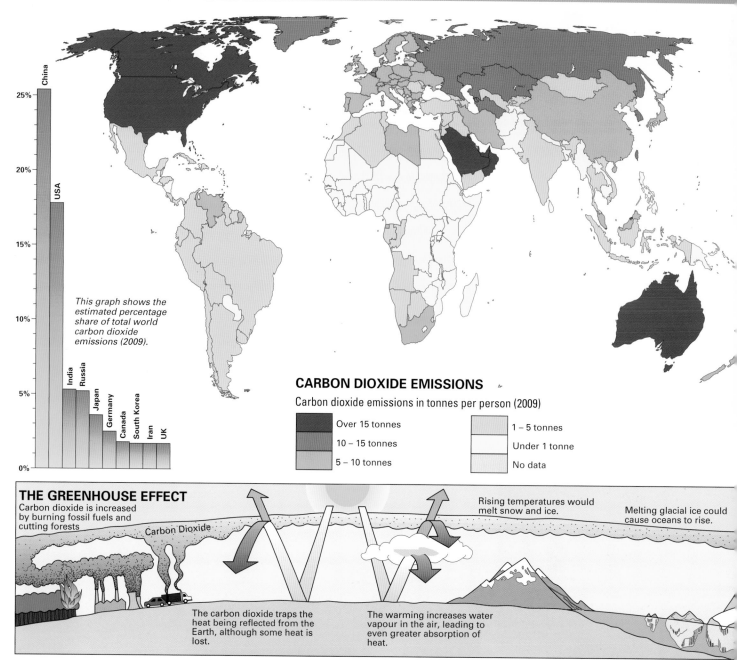

This graph shows the estimated percentage share of total world carbon dioxide emissions (2009).

(bar graph labels, left to right: China, USA, India, Russia, Japan, Germany, Canada, South Korea, Iran, UK)

CARBON DIOXIDE EMISSIONS

Carbon dioxide emissions in tonnes per person (2009)

Over 15 tonnes	1 – 5 tonnes
10 – 15 tonnes	Under 1 tonne
5 – 10 tonnes	No data

THE GREENHOUSE EFFECT

Carbon dioxide is increased by burning fossil fuels and cutting forests

Carbon Dioxide

Rising temperatures would melt snow and ice.

Melting glacial ice could cause oceans to rise.

The carbon dioxide traps the heat being reflected from the Earth, although some heat is lost.

The warming increases water vapour in the air, leading to even greater absorption of heat.

▲ Larsen B ice shelf, Antarctica. Between January and March 2002, Larsen B ice shelf on the Antarctic Peninsula collapsed. The image on the left shows its area before the collapse, while the image on the right shows the area after the collapse. The 200 m thick ice sheet had been retreating before this date, but over 500 billion tonnes of ice collapsed in under a month. This was due to rising temperatures of 0.5°C per year in this part of Antarctica. Satellite images like these ar the only way for scientists to monitor inaccessible areas of the worl

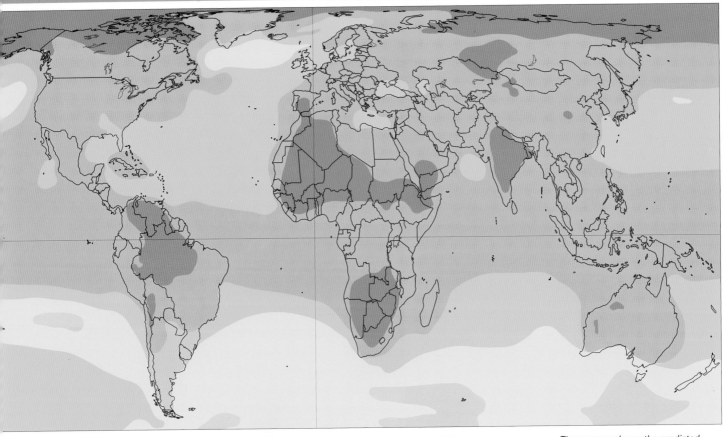

PREDICTED CHANGE IN TEMPERATURE

The difference between actual annual average surface air temperature, 1969–1990, and predicted annual average surface air temperature, 2070–2100

	5 – 10°C warmer		1 – 2°C warmer
	3 – 5°C warmer		0 – 1°C warmer
	2 – 3°C warmer		

These maps shows the predicted increase assuming a 'medium growth' of the global economy and assuming that no measures to combat the emission of greenhouse gases are taken.

It should be noted that these predicted annual average changes mask quite significant seasonal detail.

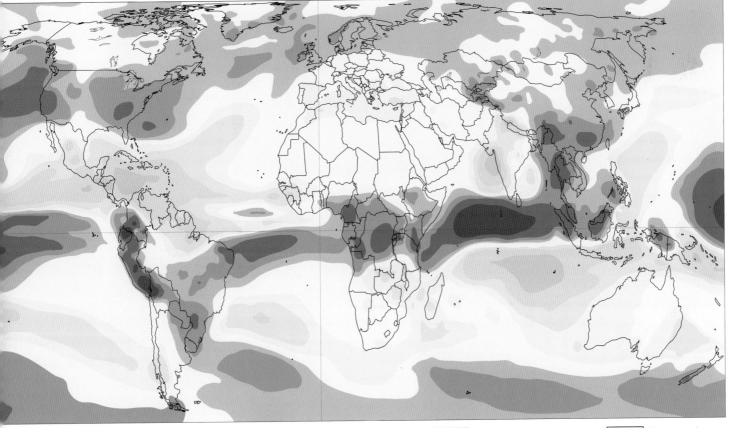

PREDICTED CHANGE IN RAINFALL

The difference between actual annual average rainfall, 1969–1990, and predicted annual average rainfall, 2070–2100

Source: The Hadley Centre of Climate Prediction and Research, Met Office

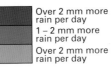

	Over 2 mm more rain per day		0.2 – 0.5 mm more rain per day		0.5 – 1 mm less rain per day
	1 – 2 mm more rain per day		No change		1 – 2 mm less rain per day
	Over 2 mm more rain per day		0.2 – 0.5 mm less rain per day		Over 2 mm less rain per day

TUNDRA AND MOUNTAIN VEGETATION

NEEDLELEAF EVERGREEN FOREST

MID-LATITUDE GRASSLAND

TROPICAL BROADLEAF RAINFOREST

DESERT

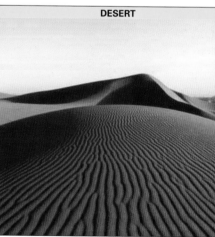

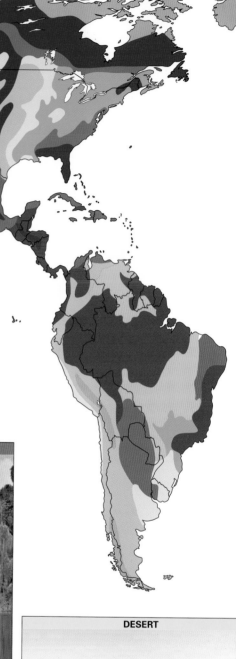

DESERTIFICATION

Existing desert

Areas with a high risk of desertification

Areas with a moderate risk of desertification

Desertification is the process by which a desert gradually spreads into neighbouring areas of semi-desert. It is usually the result of human activity, such as overgrazing by livestock.

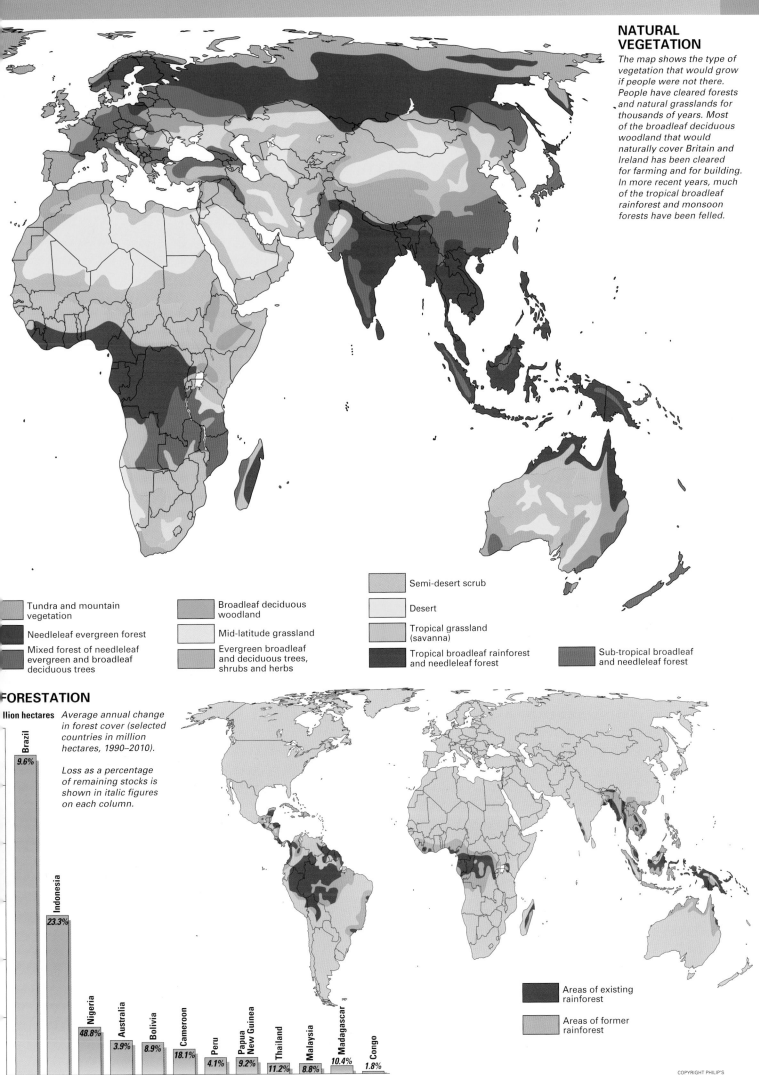

NATURAL VEGETATION

The map shows the type of vegetation that would grow if people were not there. People have cleared forests and natural grasslands for thousands of years. Most of the broadleaf deciduous woodland that would naturally cover Britain and Ireland has been cleared for farming and for building. In more recent years, much of the tropical broadleaf rainforest and monsoon forests have been felled.

Tundra and mountain vegetation

Needleleaf evergreen forest

Mixed forest of needleleaf evergreen and broadleaf deciduous trees

Broadleaf deciduous woodland

Mid-latitude grassland

Evergreen broadleaf and deciduous trees, shrubs and herbs

Semi-desert scrub

Desert

Tropical grassland (savanna)

Tropical broadleaf rainforest and needleleaf forest

Sub-tropical broadleaf and needleleaf forest

FORESTATION

llion hectares   *Average annual change in forest cover (selected countries in million hectares, 1990–2010).*

Loss as a percentage of remaining stocks is shown in italic figures on each column.

Brazil *9.6%*

Indonesia *23.3%*

Nigeria *48.8%*

Australia *3.9%*

Bolivia *8.9%*

Cameroon *18.1%*

Peru *4.1%*

Papua New Guinea *9.2%*

Thailand *11.2%*

Malaysia *8.8%*

Madagascar *10.4%*

Congo *1.8%*

Areas of existing rainforest

Areas of former rainforest

COPYRIGHT PHILIP'S

CONTINENTAL DRIFT

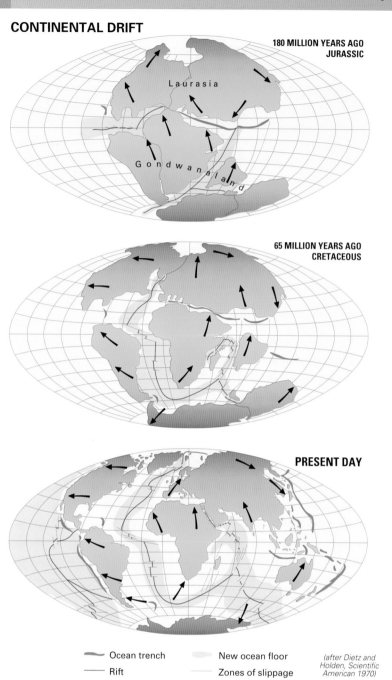

180 MILLION YEARS AGO
JURASSIC

Laurasia

Gondwanaland

65 MILLION YEARS AGO
CRETACEOUS

PRESENT DAY

— Ocean trench   New ocean floor   *(after Dietz and Holden, Scientific American 1970)*
— Rift   Zones of slippage

▲ In 1995, after almost 400 years lying dormant, the Soufrière Hills volcano on the Caribbean island of Montserrat began a series of eruptions. Further eruption in 1996 and 1997 left the south of the island uninhabitable and 5,000 people had to be evacuated to the northern zone. Steam can be seen rising from the volcano in the false colour satellite image, above.

SOUFRIÈRE HILLS VOLCANO, MONTSERRAT

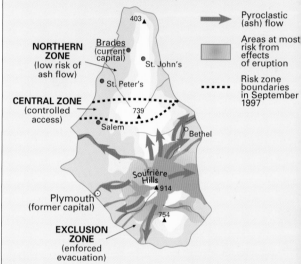

403 ▲

NORTHERN ZONE (low risk of ash flow)

Brades (current capital)

St. John's

St. Peter's

CENTRAL ZONE (controlled access)

739 ▲

Salem

Bethel

Soufrière Hills
▲ 914

Plymouth (former capital)

754 ▲

EXCLUSION ZONE (enforced evacuation)

→ Pyroclastic (ash) flow

Areas at most risk from effects of eruption

···· Risk zone boundaries in September 1997

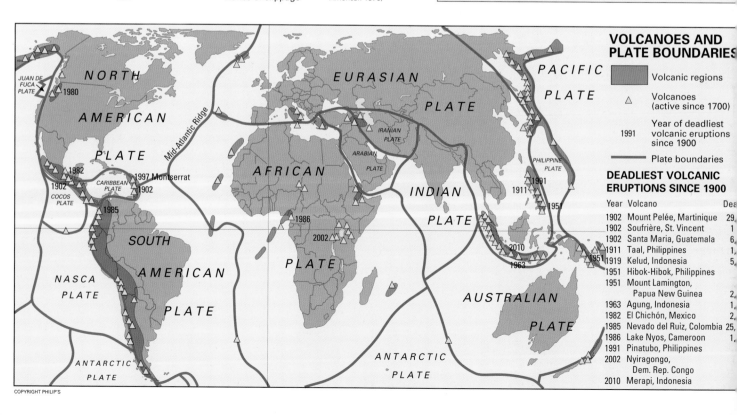

VOLCANOES AND PLATE BOUNDARIES

Volcanic regions

△ Volcanoes (active since 1700)

1991 Year of deadliest volcanic eruptions since 1900

— Plate boundaries

DEADLIEST VOLCANIC ERUPTIONS SINCE 1900

Year	Volcano	Dea
1902	Mount Pelée, Martinique	29,
1902	Soufrière, St. Vincent	1
1902	Santa Maria, Guatemala	6,
1911	Taal, Philippines	1,
1919	Kelud, Indonesia	5,
1951	Hibok-Hibok, Philippines	
1951	Mount Lamington, Papua New Guinea	2,
1963	Agung, Indonesia	1,
1982	El Chichón, Mexico	2,
1985	Nevado del Ruiz, Colombia	25,
1986	Lake Nyos, Cameroon	1,
1991	Pinatubo, Philippines	
2002	Nyiragongo, Dem. Rep. Congo	
2010	Merapi, Indonesia	

NORTH AMERICAN PLATE

JUAN DE FUCA PLATE

1980

CARIBBEAN PLATE

COCOS PLATE

1997 Montserrat

1902

1902

1985

NASCA PLATE

SOUTH AMERICAN PLATE

ANTARCTIC PLATE

Mid-Atlantic Ridge

AFRICAN PLATE

EURASIAN PLATE

IRANIAN PLATE

ARABIAN PLATE

INDIAN PLATE

AUSTRALIAN PLATE

PACIFIC PLATE

PHILIPPINE PLATE

1991

1911

1951

2010

1963

1951

1986

2002

ANTARCTIC PLATE

COPYRIGHT PHILIP'S

[PLA]TE TECTONICS IN THE CARIBBEAN

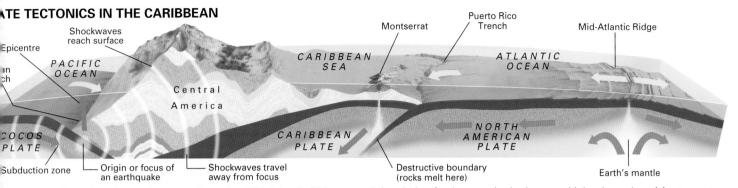

Labels on diagram: Epicentre · Shockwaves reach surface · PACIFIC OCEAN · [Ocean] · [Tren]ch · Central America · COCOS PLATE · Subduction zone · Origin or focus of an earthquake · Shockwaves travel away from focus · CARIBBEAN SEA · Montserrat · Puerto Rico Trench · ATLANTIC OCEAN · Mid-Atlantic Ridge · CARIBBEAN PLATE · NORTH AMERICAN PLATE · Destructive boundary (rocks melt here) · Earth's mantle

[The] North American Plate is moving away from the Mid-Atlantic Ridge [and] towards the Caribbean Plate at a rate of 30-40mm a year. The [edg]e of the North American Plate is forced downwards under the [Carib]bean Plate. As the North American Plate descends, the rocks melt [and] are destroyed. This is called a *destructive boundary*. The destructive [boun]dary to the east of the Caribbean has caused the Puerto Rico Trench and the chain of volcanoes in the Leeward Islands such as Montserrat. The molten rocks along the destructive boundary are forced upwards through cracks at the edge of the Caribbean Plate to pour out as lava from volcanoes. Earthquakes are also common along destructive plate boundaries, as is the case in Central America, along the boundary between the Caribbean and Cocos Plates.

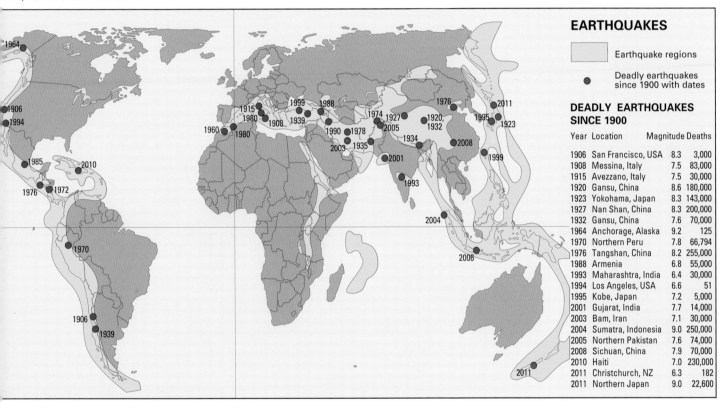

EARTHQUAKES

Earthquake regions

• Deadly earthquakes since 1900 with dates

DEADLY EARTHQUAKES SINCE 1900

Year	Location	Magnitude	Deaths
1906	San Francisco, USA	8.3	3,000
1908	Messina, Italy	7.5	83,000
1915	Avezzano, Italy	7.5	30,000
1920	Gansu, China	8.6	180,000
1923	Yokohama, Japan	8.3	143,000
1927	Nan Shan, China	8.3	200,000
1932	Gansu, China	7.6	70,000
1964	Anchorage, Alaska	9.2	125
1970	Northern Peru	7.8	66,794
1976	Tangshan, China	8.2	255,000
1988	Armenia	6.8	55,000
1993	Maharashtra, India	6.4	30,000
1994	Los Angeles, USA	6.6	51
1995	Kobe, Japan	7.2	5,000
2001	Gujarat, India	7.7	14,000
2003	Bam, Iran	7.1	30,000
2004	Sumatra, Indonesia	9.0	250,000
2005	Northern Pakistan	7.6	74,000
2008	Sichuan, China	7.9	70,000
2010	Haiti	7.0	230,000
2011	Christchurch, NZ	6.3	182
2011	Northern Japan	9.0	22,600

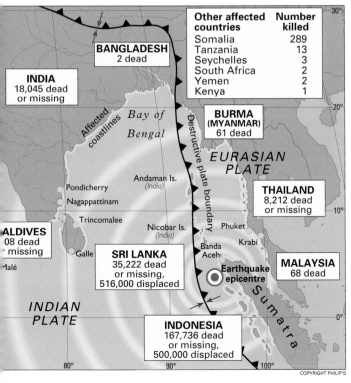

Map labels: BANGLADESH 2 dead · INDIA 18,045 dead or missing · Affected coastlines · Bay of Bengal · Pondicherry · Nagappattinam · Trincomalee · Andaman Is. (India) · Destructive plate boundary · EURASIAN PLATE · Nicobar Is. (India) · BURMA (MYANMAR) 61 dead · THAILAND 8,212 dead or missing · Phuket · Krabi · [M]ALDIVES [1]08 dead [or] missing · Malé · Galle · Banda Aceh · SRI LANKA 35,222 dead or missing, 516,000 displaced · MALAYSIA 68 dead · Earthquake epicentre · INDIAN PLATE · Sumatra · INDONESIA 167,736 dead or missing, 500,000 displaced

Other affected countries	Number killed
Somalia	289
Tanzania	13
Seychelles	3
South Africa	2
Yemen	2
Kenya	1

INDIAN OCEAN TSUNAMI

On 26 December 2004, an earthquake off the coast of Sumatra triggered a deadly tsunami that swept across the Indian Ocean, causing devastation in many countries (see map left).
The image below shows the turbulent receding waters of the tsunami, on the west coast of Sri Lanka. Such imagery enabled rescuers to assess the worst affected areas.

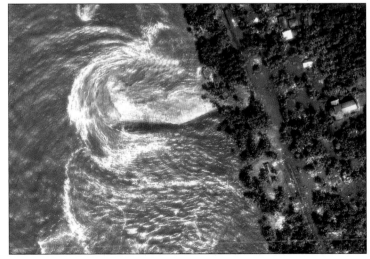

POPULATION DENSITY BY COUNTRY

Density of people per square kilometre (2012)

250 per km² and over

100 – 250 per km²

50 – 100 per km²

10 – 50 per km²

Under 10 per km²

No data

Most and least densely populated countries

Most per km²		Least per km²	
Monaco	15,646	W. Sahara	2
Singapore	7,725	Mongolia	2
Gaza Strip	4,751	Australia	3
Samoa	3,186	Namibia	3
Bahrain	1,877	Suriname	3

UK 258 per km²

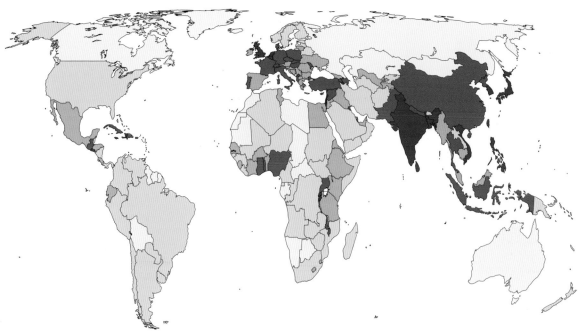

POPULATION CHANGE

Expected change in total population (2004–2050)

Over 125% gain

100 – 125% gain

50 – 100% gain

25 – 50% gain

0 – 25% gain

No change or loss

Based on estimates for the year 2050, the ten most populous nations in the world will be, in millions:

India	1,628	Pakistan	295
China	1,437	Bangladesh	280
USA	420	Brazil	221
Indonesia	308	Congo Dem. Rep.	181
Nigeria	307	Ethiopia	171

UK (2050) 77 million

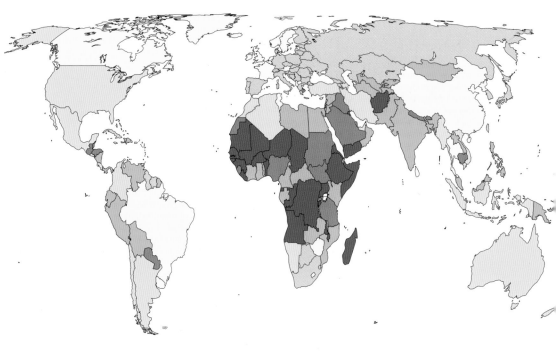

URBAN POPULATION

Percentage of total population living in towns and cities (2010)

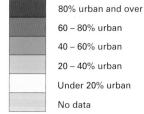

80% urban and over

60 – 80% urban

40 – 60% urban

20 – 40% urban

Under 20% urban

No data

Countries that are the most and least urbanized (%)

Most urbanized		Least urbanized	
Singapore	100	Burundi	11
Kuwait	98	Papua N. Guinea	13
Belgium	97	Uganda	13

UK 80% urban

In 2008, for the first time in history, more than half the world's population lived in urban areas.

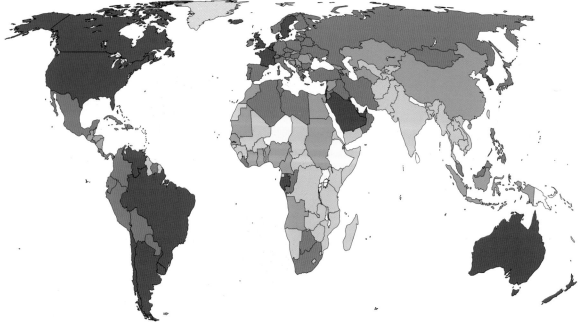

POPULATION BY CONTINENT

In this diagram the size of each continent is in proportion to its population (2011).

Each square represents 10 million people.

Population of countries (2012)
Top 20 countries (millions)

China	1,343
India	1,205
USA	314
Indonesia	249
Brazil	199
Pakistan	190
Nigeria	170
Bangladesh	161
Russia	143
Japan	127
Mexico	115
Philippines	104
Vietnam	92
Ethiopia	91
Egypt	84
Germany	81
Turkey	80
Iran	79
Congo, Dem. Rep.	74
Thailand	67

UK 63 million

LIFE EXPECTANCY

The average expected lifespan of babies born in 2010

- Over 80 years
- 70 – 80 years
- 60 – 70 years
- 50 – 60 years
- Under 50 years
- No data

Countries with the highest and lowest life expectancy at birth in years

Highest		Lowest	
Australia	82	Angola	39
Italy	82	Afghanistan	45
Japan	82	Nigeria	48
Singapore	82	Chad	48
Canada	81	South Africa	49

UK 80 years

WEALTH

The value of total production in 2010 divided by the population (the Gross National Income per capita)

- Over 400% of world average
- 200 – 400% of world average
- 100 – 200% of world average

World average wealth per person $9,135

- 50 – 100% of world average
- 25 – 50% of world average
- 10 – 25% of world average
- Under 10% of world average
- No data

Top 3 countries		Bottom 3 countries	
Monaco	$183,150	Burundi	$170
Liechtenstein	$137,070	Congo (D. Rep.)	$180
Norway	$87,350	Liberia	$200

UK $38,000

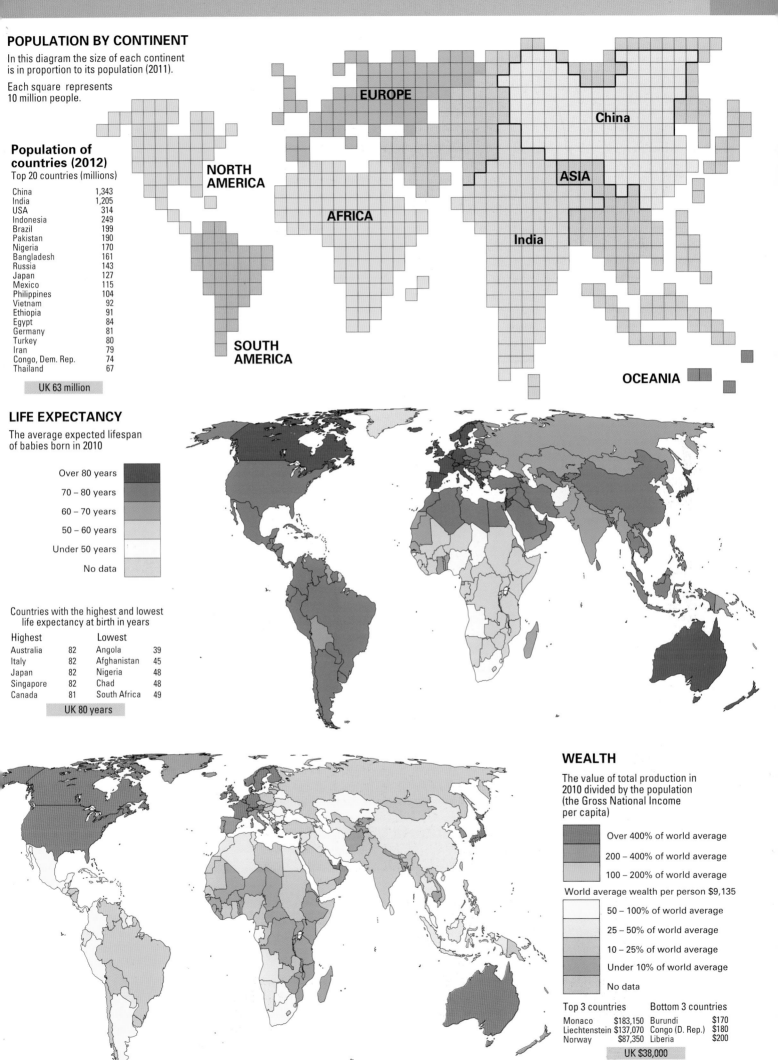

COPYRIGHT PHILIP'S

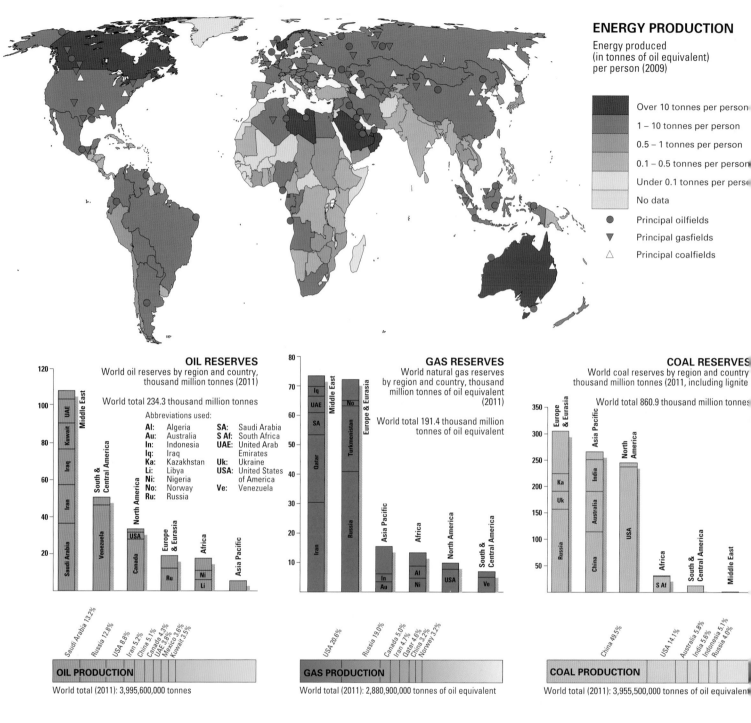

ENERGY PRODUCTION

Energy produced
(in tonnes of oil equivalent)
per person (2009)

- Over 10 tonnes per person
- 1 – 10 tonnes per person
- 0.5 – 1 tonnes per person
- 0.1 – 0.5 tonnes per person
- Under 0.1 tonnes per person
- No data

- ● Principal oilfields
- ▼ Principal gasfields
- △ Principal coalfields

OIL RESERVES

World oil reserves by region and country,
thousand million tonnes (2011)

World total 234.3 thousand million tonnes

Abbreviations used:

Al:	Algeria	**SA:**	Saudi Arabia
Au:	Australia	**S Af:**	South Africa
In:	Indonesia	**UAE:**	United Arab Emirates
Iq:	Iraq		
Ka:	Kazakhstan	**Uk:**	Ukraine
Li:	Libya	**USA:**	United States of America
Ni:	Nigeria		
No:	Norway	**Ve:**	Venezuela
Ru:	Russia		

OIL PRODUCTION

Saudi Arabia 13.2% Russia 12.8% USA 8.8% Iran 5.2% China 5.1% Canada 4.3% UAE 3.8% Mexico 3.6% Kuwait 3.5%

World total (2011): 3,995,600,000 tonnes

GAS RESERVES

World natural gas reserves
by region and country, thousand
million tonnes of oil equivalent
(2011)

World total 191.4 thousand million
tonnes of oil equivalent

GAS PRODUCTION

USA 20.6% Russia 19.0% Canada 5.0% Iran 4.7% Qatar 4.6% China 3.2% Norway 3.2%

World total (2011): 2,880,900,000 tonnes of oil equivalent

COAL RESERVES

World coal reserves by region and country
thousand million tonnes (2011, including lignite)

World total 860.9 thousand million tonnes

COAL PRODUCTION

China 49.5% USA 14.1% Australia 5.8% India 5.6% Indonesia 5.1% Russia 4.0%

World total (2011): 3,955,500,000 tonnes of oil equivalent

ELECTRICITY PRODUCTION

Percentage of electricity
generated by source (2010)

- Over 75% from thermal
- 50 – 75% from thermal
- over 75% from hydro
- 50 – 75% from hydro
- Over 50% from nuclear
- No dominant source
- No data

- ● Principal geothermal plants
- ◆ Principal hydroelectric plants

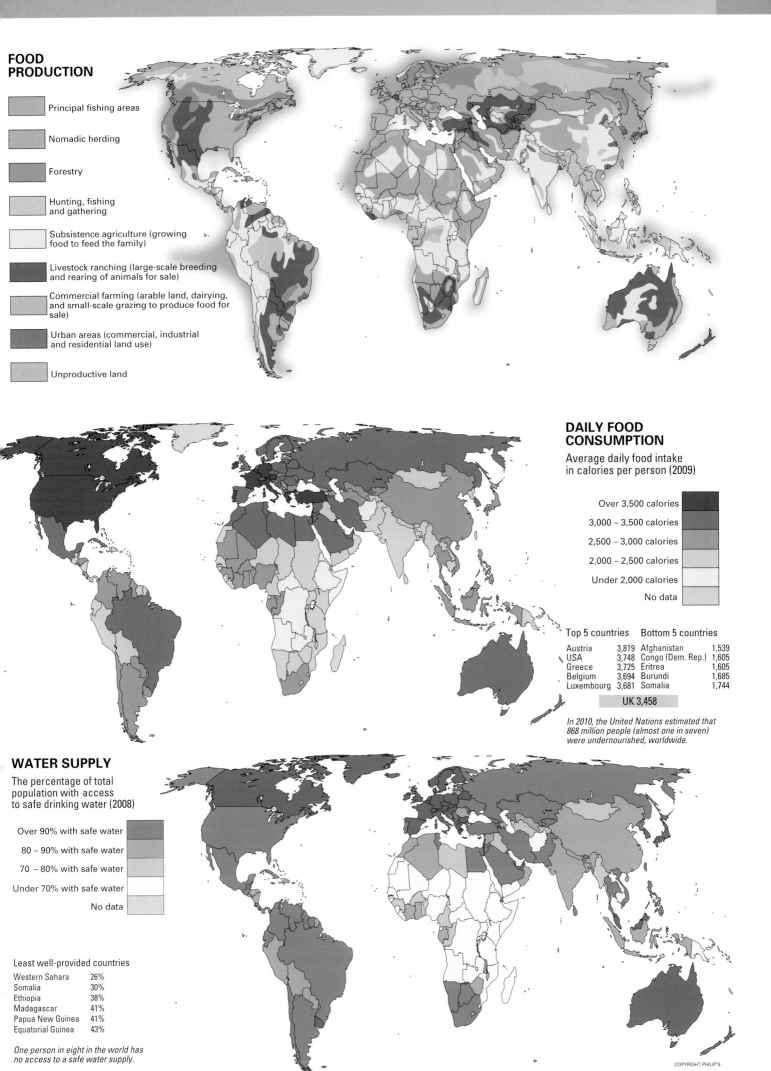

FOOD PRODUCTION

- Principal fishing areas
- Nomadic herding
- Forestry
- Hunting, fishing and gathering
- Subsistence agriculture (growing food to feed the family)
- Livestock ranching (large-scale breeding and rearing of animals for sale)
- Commercial farming (arable land, dairying, and small-scale grazing to produce food for sale)
- Urban areas (commercial, industrial and residential land use)
- Unproductive land

DAILY FOOD CONSUMPTION

Average daily food intake in calories per person (2009)

- Over 3,500 calories
- 3,000 – 3,500 calories
- 2,500 – 3,000 calories
- 2,000 – 2,500 calories
- Under 2,000 calories
- No data

Top 5 countries		Bottom 5 countries	
Austria	3,819	Afghanistan	1,539
USA	3,748	Congo (Dem. Rep.)	1,605
Greece	3,725	Eritrea	1,605
Belgium	3,694	Burundi	1,685
Luxembourg	3,681	Somalia	1,744

| UK 3,458 |

In 2010, the United Nations estimated that 868 million people (almost one in seven) were undernourished, worldwide.

WATER SUPPLY

The percentage of total population with access to safe drinking water (2008)

- Over 90% with safe water
- 80 – 90% with safe water
- 70 – 80% with safe water
- Under 70% with safe water
- No data

Least well-provided countries

Western Sahara	26%
Somalia	30%
Ethiopia	38%
Madagascar	41%
Papua New Guinea	41%
Equatorial Guinea	43%

One person in eight in the world has no access to a safe water supply.

WORLD TRADE

The percentage share of total
world exports by value (2011)

- Over 10%
- 5 – 10%
- 2.5 – 5%
- 1.0 – 2.5%
- 0.1 – 1.0%
- Under 0.1%
- No data

☆ Member of 'G8'

*The members of 'G8' account
for more than half the total trade.
The majority of nations contribute
less than one quarter of 1% to
the worldwide total of exports;
EU countries account for over 30%;
the Pacific Rim nations over 45%.*

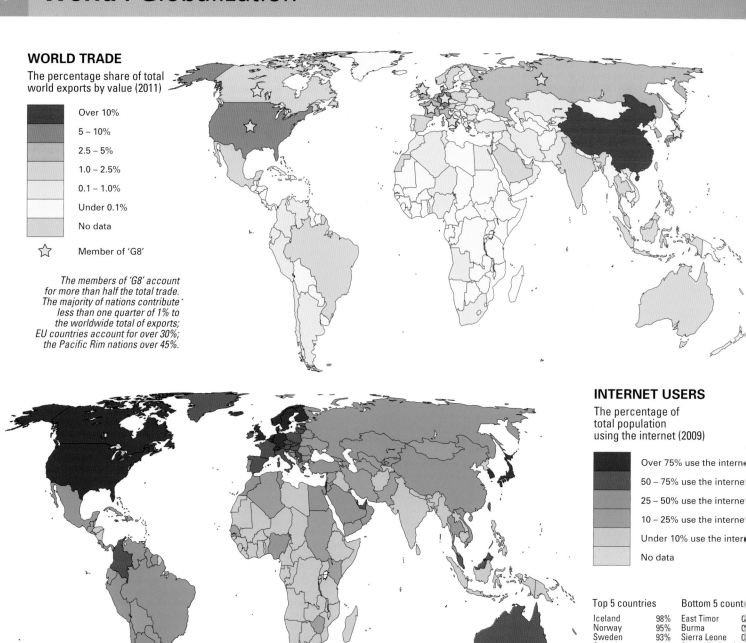

INTERNET USERS

The percentage of
total population
using the internet (2009)

- Over 75% use the intern
- 50 – 75% use the interne
- 25 – 50% use the interne
- 10 – 25% use the interne
- Under 10% use the inter
- No data

Top 5 countries		Bottom 5 count	
Iceland	98%	East Timor	C
Norway	95%	Burma	C
Sweden	93%	Sierra Leone	C
St Lucia	89%	Congo (D. Rep.)	0
Netherlands	89%	Bangladesh	0

UK 84%

INTERNATIONAL AID

Official Development
Assistance (ODA) provided
and received, US$ per
person (2010)

- Over $250
- $100 – $250   ↑
- $50 – $100   PROVIDERS

- Under $10   RECEIVERS
- $10 – $50
- $50 – $100   ↓
- Over $100
- No data

Top 5 providers		Top 5 receivers	
Norway	$975	Tuvalu	$1,785
Luxembourg	$806	Palau	$1,737
Denmark	$522	Marshall Is	$1,101
Sweden	$498	Micronesia	$1,093
Netherlands	$378	Gaza Strip	$748

UK provides $208

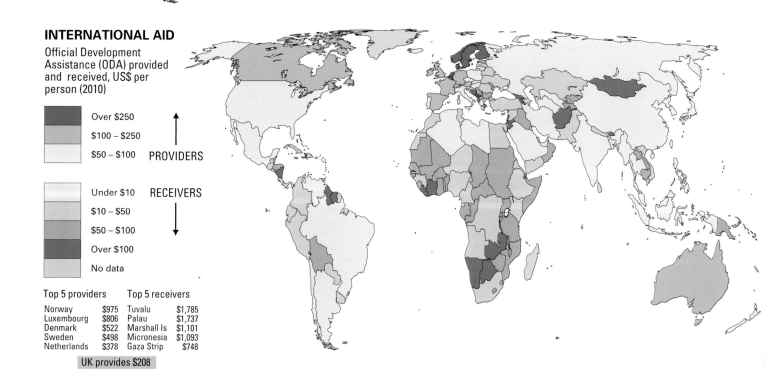

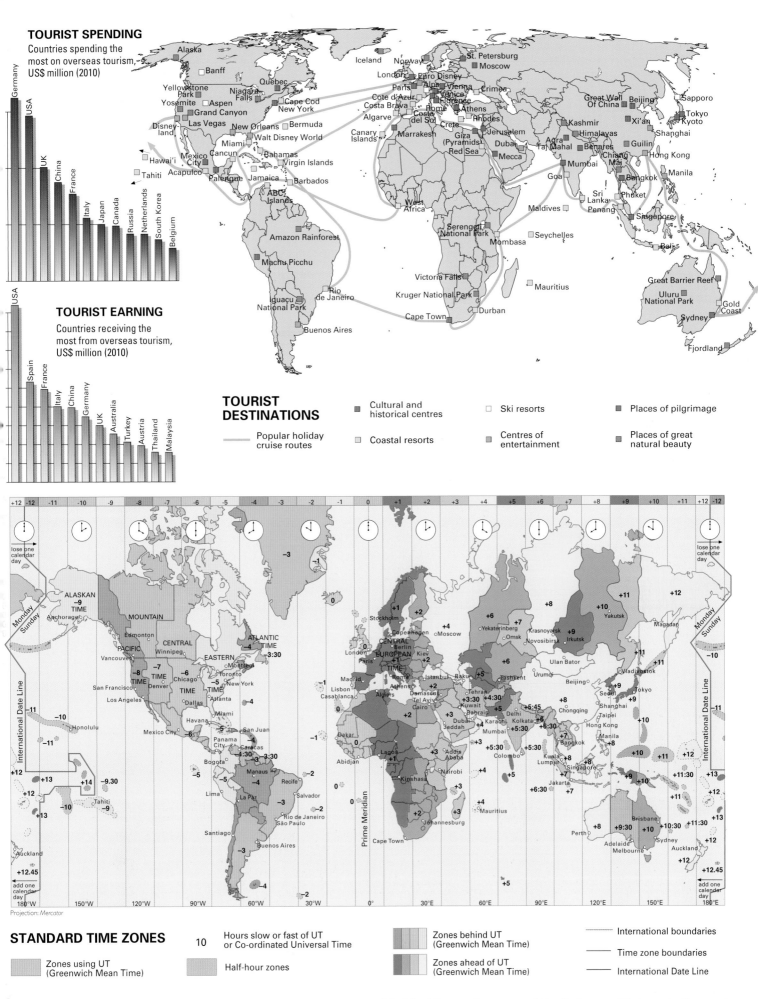

TOURIST SPENDING

Countries spending the most on overseas tourism, US$ million (2010)

Germany, USA, UK, China, France, Italy, Japan, Canada, Russia, Netherlands, South Korea, Belgium

TOURIST EARNING

Countries receiving the most from overseas tourism, US$ million (2010)

USA, Spain, France, Italy, China, Germany, UK, Australia, Turkey, Austria, Thailand, Malaysia

TOURIST DESTINATIONS

— Popular holiday cruise routes

■ Cultural and historical centres
□ Coastal resorts
□ Ski resorts
■ Centres of entertainment
■ Places of pilgrimage
■ Places of great natural beauty

STANDARD TIME ZONES

10   Hours slow or fast of UT or Co-ordinated Universal Time

Zones using UT (Greenwich Mean Time)
Half-hour zones
Zones behind UT (Greenwich Mean Time)
Zones ahead of UT (Greenwich Mean Time)

------ International boundaries
—— Time zone boundaries
—— International Date Line

Projection: Mercator

The Earth rotates through 360° in 24 hours, and so moves 15° every hour. The World is divided into 24 standard time zones, each centred on lines of longitude at 15° intervals. The Greenwich Meridian (or Prime Meridian) lies on the centre of the first zone. All places to the west of Greenwich are one hour behind for every 15° of longitude; places to the east are ahead by one hour for every 15°.

FLAG	COUNTRY	CAPITAL CITY	AREA thousand square kilometres 2012	POPULATION million people 2012	POPULATION CHANGE percent per year 2012	BIRTHS per thousand people 2012	DEATHS per thousand people 2012	LIFE EXPECTANCY years 2012	INCOME US $ per person 2011
	Afghanistan	Kabul	652	30.4	2.2	39	15	50	1,000
	Albania	Tirane	28.7	3.0	0.3	12	6	78	7,800
	Algeria	Algiers	2,382	37.4	1.9	24	4	75	7,200
	Angola	Luanda	1,247	18.1	2.8	39	12	55	5,900
	Argentina	Buenos Aires	2,780	42.2	1.0	17	7	77	17,400
	Armenia	Yerevan	29.8	3.0	0.1	13	8	73	5,400
	Australia	Canberra	7,741	22.0	1.1	12	7	82	40,800
	Austria	Vienna	83.9	8.2	0.0	9	10	80	41,700
	Azerbaijan	Baku	86.6	9.5	1.0	17	7	71	10,200
	Bahamas	Nassau	13.9	0.3	0.9	16	7	71	30,900
	Bahrain	Manama	0.7	1.2	2.7	14	3	78	27,300
	Bangladesh	Dhaka	144	161.1	1.6	23	6	70	1,700
	Barbados	Bridgetown	0.4	0.3	0.4	12	8	75	23,600
	Belarus	Minsk	208	9.6	-0.2	11	14	71	14,900
	Belgium	Brussels	30.5	10.4	0.1	10	11	80	37,600
	Belize	Belmopan	23.0	0.3	2.0	26	6	68	8,300
	Benin	Porto-Novo	113	9.6	2.9	38	9	60	1,500
	Bhutan	Thimphu	47.0	0.7	1.2	19	7	68	6,000
	Bolivia	La Paz/Sucre	1,099	10.3	1.7	24	7	68	4,800
	Bosnia-Herzegovina	Sarajevo	51.2	3.9	-0.1	9	9	79	8,200
	Botswana	Gaborone	582	2.1	1.5	22	12	56	16,300
	Brazil	Brasília	8,514	199.3	0.9	15	7	73	11,600
	Brunei	Bandar Seri Begawan	5.8	0.4	1.7	18	3	76	49,400
	Bulgaria	Sofia	111	7.0	-0.8	9	14	74	13,500
	Burkina Faso	Ouagadougou	274	17.3	3.1	43	12	54	1,500
	Burma	Rangoon/Naypyidaw	677	54.6	1.1	19	8	65	1,300
	Burundi	Bujumbura	27.8	10.6	3.1	41	9	59	400
	Cambodia	Phnom Penh	181	15.0	1.7	25	8	63	2,300
	Cameroon	Yaoundé	475	20.1	2.1	32	12	55	2,300
	Canada	Ottawa	9,971	34.3	0.8	10	8	81	40,300
	Cape Verde Islands	Praia	4.0	0.5	1.4	21	6	71	4,000
	Central African Republic	Bangui	623	5.1	2.1	36	15	50	800
	Chad	N'djamena	1,284	11.0	2.0	39	15	49	1,900
	Chile	Santiago	757	17.1	0.9	14	6	78	16,100
	China	Beijing	9,597	1343.2	0.5	12	7	75	8,400
	Colombia	Bogotá	1,139	45.2	1.1	17	5	75	10,100
	Congo	Brazzaville	342	4.4	2.8	40	11	55	4,600
	Congo (Dem. Rep.)	Kinshasa	2,345	73.6	2.6	37	11	56	300
	Costa Rica	San José	51.1	4.6	1.3	16	4	78	11,500
	Croatia	Zagreb	56.5	4.5	-0.1	10	12	76	18,300
	Cuba	Havana	111	11.1	-0.1	10	8	78	9,900
	Cyprus	Nicosia	9.3	1.1	1.6	11	6	78	29,100
	Czech Republic	Prague	78.9	10.2	-0.1	9	11	77	25,900

FLAG	COUNTRY	CAPITAL CITY	AREA thousand square kilometres 2012	POPULATION million people 2012	POPULATION CHANGE percent per year 2012	BIRTHS per thousand people 2012	DEATHS per thousand people 2012	LIFE EXPECTANCY years 2012	INCOME US $ per person 2011
	Denmark	Copenhagen	43.1	5.5	0.2	10	10	79	40,200
	Djibouti	Djibouti	23.2	0.8	2.3	25	8	62	2,600
	Dominican Republic	Santo Domingo	48.5	10.1	1.3	19	4	77	9,300
	East Timor	Dili	14.9	1.1	2.5	35	6	68	3,100
	Ecuador	Quito	284	15.2	1.4	20	5	76	8,300
	Egypt	Cairo	1,001	83.7	1.9	24	5	73	6,500
	El Salvador	San Salvador	21.0	6.1	0.3	17	6	74	7,600
	Equatorial Guinea	Malabo	28.1	0.7	2.6	35	9	63	19,300
	Eritrea	Asmara	118	6.1	2.5	32	8	63	700
	Estonia	Tallinn	45.1	1.3	-0.7	10	14	74	20,200
	Ethiopia	Addis Ababa	1,104	91.2	2.9	39	9	57	1,100
	Fiji	Suva	18.3	0.9	0.8	21	6	72	4,600
	Finland	Helsinki	338	5.3	0.1	10	10	79	38,300
	France	Paris	552	65.6	0.5	13	9	81	35,000
	Gabon	Libreville	268	1.6	2.0	35	13	52	16,000
	Gambia	Banjul	11.3	1.8	2.3	33	8	64	2,100
	Georgia	Tbilisi	69.7	4.6	-0.3	11	10	77	5,400
	Germany	Berlin	357	81.3	-0.2	8	11	80	37,900
	Ghana	Accra	239	24.7	2.2	32	8	61	3,100
	Greece	Athens	132	10.8	0.1	9	11	80	27,600
	Guatemala	Guatemala	109	14.1	1.9	26	5	71	5,000
	Guinea	Conakry	246	10.9	2.6	37	10	59	1,100
	Guinea-Bissau	Bissau	36.1	1.6	2.0	35	15	49	1,100
	Guyana	Georgetown	215	0.7	-0.3	17	7	67	7,500
	Haiti	Port-au-Prince	27.8	9.8	0.9	24	8	63	1,200
	Honduras	Tegucigalpa	112	8.3	1.8	25	5	71	4,300
	Hungary	Budapest	93.0	10.0	-0.2	9	13	75	19,600
	Iceland	Reykjavik	103	0.3	0.7	13	7	81	38,000
	India	New Delhi	3,287	1,205.1	1.3	21	7	67	3,700
	Indonesia	Jakarta	1,905	248.6	1.0	18	6	72	4,700
	Iran	Tehrān	1,648	78.9	1.2	19	6	70	12,200
	Iraq	Baghdād	438	31.1	2.3	28	5	71	3,900
	Ireland	Dublin	70.3	4.7	1.1	16	6	80	39,500
	Israel	Jerusalem	20.6	7.6	1.5	19	6	81	31,000
	Italy	Rome	301	61.3	0.4	9	10	82	30,100
	Ivory Coast	Yamoussoukro	322	22.0	2.0	30	10	57	1,600
	Jamaica	Kingston	11.0	2.9	0.7	19	7	73	9,000
	Japan	Tokyo	378	127.4	-0.1	8	9	84	34,300
	Jordan	Amman	89.3	6.5	-1.0	27	3	80	5,900
	Kazakhstan	Astana	2,725	17.5	1.2	20	9	70	13,000
	Kenya	Nairobi	580	43.0	2.4	32	7	63	1,700
	Korea, North	P'yŏngyang	121	24.6	0.5	15	9	69	1,800
	Korea, South	Seoul	99.3	48.9	0.2	8	6	79	31,700

FLAG	COUNTRY	CAPITAL CITY	AREA thousand square kilometres 2012	POPULATION million people 2012	POPULATION CHANGE percent per year 2012	BIRTHS per thousand people 2012	DEATHS per thousand people 2012	LIFE EXPECTANCY years 2012	INCOME US $ per person 2011
	Kosovo	Priština	10.9	1.8	-	-	-	75	6,500
	Kuwait	Kuwait	17.8	2.6	1.9	21	2	77	40,700
	Kyrgyzstan	Bishkek	200	5.5	0.9	24	7	69	2,400
	Laos	Vientiane	237	6.6	1.7	26	8	63	2,700
	Latvia	Riga	64.6	2.2	-0.6	10	14	73	15,400
	Lebanon	Beirut	10.4	4.1	-0.4	15	7	75	15,600
	Lesotho	Maseru	30.4	1.9	0.3	27	15	52	1,400
	Liberia	Monrovia	111	3.9	2.6	36	10	57	400
	Libya	Tripoli	1,760	5.6	2.0	18	5	78	14,100
	Lithuania	Vilnius	65.2	3.5	-0.3	9	11	76	18,700
	Luxembourg	Luxembourg	2.6	0.5	1.1	12	9	80	84,700
	Macedonia	Skopje	25.7	2.1	0.2	12	9	75	10,400
	Madagascar	Antananarivo	587	22.0	2.7	34	7	64	900
	Malawi	Lilongwe	118	16.3	2.8	40	13	52	900
	Malaysia	Kuala Lumpur/ Putrajaya	330	29.2	1.5	21	5	74	15,600
	Mali	Bamako	1,240	15.5	3.0	47	14	53	1,300
	Malta	Valletta	0.3	0.4	0.4	10	9	80	25,700
	Mauritania	Nouakchott	1,026	3.4	2.3	33	9	62	2,200
	Mauritius	Port Louis	2.0	1.3	0.7	14	7	75	15,000
	Mexico	Mexico City	1,958	115.0	1.1	19	5	77	15,100
	Moldova	Kishinev	33.9	3.7	-1.0	13	13	70	3,400
	Mongolia	Ulan Bator	1,567	3.2	1.5	21	6	90	4,500
	Montenegro	Podgorica	14.0	0.7	-0.6	11	9	69	11,200
	Morocco	Rabat	447	32.3	1.1	19	5	73	5,100
	Mozambique	Maputo	802	23.5	2.4	39	13	52	1,100
	Namibia	Windhoek	824	2.2	0.8	21	13	52	7,300
	Nepal	Katmandu	147	29.9	1.8	22	7	67	1,300
	Netherlands	Amsterdam/ The Hague	41.5	16.7	0.5	11	8	81	42,300
	New Zealand	Wellington	271	4.3	0.9	14	7	81	27,900
	Nicaragua	Managua	130	5.7	1.1	19	5	72	3,200
	Niger	Niamey	1,267	16.3	3.4	48	13	54	800
	Nigeria	Abuja	924	170.1	2.6	39	13	52	2,600
	Norway	Oslo	324	4.7	0.3	11	9	80	53,300
	Oman	Muscat	310	3.1	2.0	24	3	74	26,200
	Pakistan	Islamabad	796	190.3	1.6	24	7	66	2,800
	Panama	Panamá	75.5	3.5	1.4	19	5	78	13,600
	Papua New Guinea	Port Moresby	463	6.3	1.9	26	7	66	2,500
	Paraguay	Asunción	407	6.5	1.3	17	5	76	5,500
	Peru	Lima	1,285	29.6	1.0	19	6	73	10,000
	Philippines	Manila	300	103.8	1.9	25	5	72	4,100
	Poland	Warsaw	323	38.4	-0.1	10	10	76	20,100
	Portugal	Lisbon	88.8	10.8	0.2	10	11	79	23,200
	Qatar	Doha	11.0	2.0	4.9	10	2	78	102,700

FLAG	COUNTRY	CAPITAL CITY	AREA thousand square kilometres 2012	POPULATION million people 2012	POPULATION CHANGE percent per year 2012	BIRTHS per thousand people 2012	DEATHS per thousand people 2012	LIFE EXPECTANCY years 2012	INCOME US $ per person 2011
	Romania	Bucharest	238	21.8	-0.3	9	12	74	12,300
	Russia	Moscow	17,075	142.5	-0.0	12	14	66	16,700
	Rwanda	Kigali	26.3	11.7	2.8	36	10	58	1,300
	Saudi Arabia	Riyadh	2,150	26.5	1.5	19	3	74	24,000
	Senegal	Dakar	197	13.0	2.5	36	9	60	1,900
	Serbia	Belgrade	77.5	7.3	-0.5	9	14	75	10,700
	Sierra Leone	Freetown	71.7	5.5	2.3	38	11	57	800
	Singapore	Singapore	0.7	5.4	2.0	8	3	84	59,900
	Slovakia	Bratislava	49.0	5.5	0.1	10	10	76	23,400
	Slovenia	Ljubljana	20.3	2.0	-0.2	9	11	77	29,100
	Solomon Islands	Honiara	28.9	0.6	2.2	27	4	74	3,300
	Somalia	Mogadishu	638	10.1	1.6	42	15	51	600
	South Africa	Cape Town/ Pretoria	1,221	48.8	-0.4	19	17	49	11,000
	South Sudan	Juba	620	10.6	-	-	-	-	1,546
	Spain	Madrid	498	47.0	0.7	10	9	82	30,600
	Sri Lanka	Colombo	65.6	21.5	0.9	17	6	76	5,600
	Sudan	Khartoum	1,886	34.2	1.9	32	8	83	3,000
	Suriname	Paramaribo	163	0.6	1.2	17	6	71	9,500
	Swaziland	Mbabane	17.4	1.4	1.2	26	14	49	5,200
	Sweden	Stockholm	450	9.1	0.2	10	10	81	40,600
	Switzerland	Berne	41.3	7.9	0.9	10	8	81	43,400
	Syria	Damascus	185	22.5	-0.8	24	4	75	5,100
	Taiwan	Taipei	36.0	23.2	0.3	9	7	78	37,900
	Tajikistan	Dushanbe	143	7.8	1.8	26	6	66	2,000
	Tanzania	Dodoma	945	46.9	2.9	38	9	53	1,500
	Thailand	Bangkok	513	67.1	0.5	13	7	74	9,700
	Togo	Lomé	56.8	7.0	2.7	35	8	63	900
	Trinidad and Tobago	Port of Spain	5.1	1.2	-0.1	14	8	72	20,300
	Tunisia	Tunis	164	10.7	1.0	17	6	75	9,500
	Turkey	Ankara	775	79.7	1.2	18	6	73	14,600
	Turkmenistan	Ashkhabad	488	5.1	1.1	20	6	69	7,500
	Uganda	Kampala	241	33.6	3.3	46	12	53	1,300
	Ukraine	Kiev	604	44.9	-0.6	10	16	69	7,200
	United Arab Emirates	Abu Dhabi	83.6	5.3	3.1	16	2	77	48,500
	United Kingdom	London	242	63.0	0.6	12	9	80	35,900
	USA	Washington D.C.	9,629	313.8	0.9	14	8	78	48,100
	Uruguay	Montevideo	175	3.3	0.2	13	10	76	15,400
	Uzbekistan	Tashkent	447	28.4	0.9	17	5	73	3,300
	Venezuela	Caracas	912	28.0	1.5	20	5	74	12,400
	Vietnam	Hanoi	332	91.5	1.1	17	6	72	3,300
	Yemen	Sana	528	24.8	2.6	33	7	64	2,500
	Zambia	Lusaka	753	13.8	2.9	43	13	53	1,600
	Zimbabwe	Harare	391	12.6	4.4	32	12	52	500

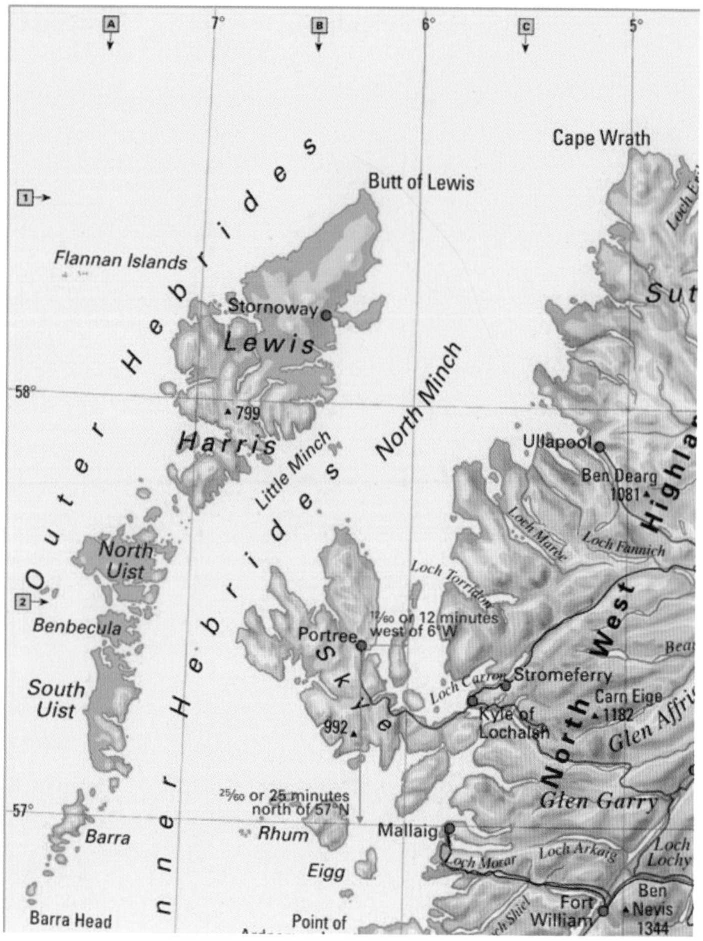
A
B
C
7°
6°
5°
1
2
58°
57°
Cape Wrath
Butt of Lewis
Flannan Islands
Stornoway
Lewis
799
Harris
North Minch
Little Minch
Outer Hebrides
Inner Hebrides
Ullapool
Ben Dearg
1081
Loch Maree
Loch Fannich
Loch Torridon
North Uist
Benbecula
12/60 or 12 minutes west of 6°W
Portree
Skye
Stromeferry
Loch Carron
Carn Eige
1182
Kyle of Lochalsh
North West Highlands
Glen Affric
South Uist
992
25/60 or 25 minutes north of 57°N
Glen Garry
Barra
Rhum
Mallaig
Loch Morar
Loch Arkaig
Loch Lochy
Eigg
Barra Head
Point of
Ben Nevis
1344
Fort William
Loch Shiel

This index contains the names of all the principal places and features shown on the maps in the atlas. They are listed in alphabetical order. If a name has a description as part of it, for example, Bay of Biscay, the name is in alphabetical order, followed by the description:

Biscay, Bay of ......

Sometimes, the same name occurs in more than one country. In these cases, the country names are added after each place name. For example:

Córdoba, *Argentina* ..
Córdoba, *Spain* .....

All rivers are indexed to their mouths or confluences and are followed by the symbol ➜. All country names are followed by the symbol ■.

Each place name is followed by its latitude and longitude, and then its map page number and figure-letter grid reference. Both latitude and longitude are measured in degrees and minutes. There are 60 minutes in a degree. The latitude is followed by N(orth) or S(outh) and the longitude by E(ast) or W(est). The map extract on the left shows how to find a place by estimating the required distance from the nearest line of latitude or longitude on the map page. Portree is used as an example:

Portree .... 57°25′N 6°12′W **18 2B**

There are 60 minutes between the lines and so to find the position of Portree an estimate has to be made. 25 parts of the 60 minutes north of the 57°N latitude line, and 12 parts of the 60 minutes west of the 6°W longitude line.

The latitude and longitude are followed by a number in bold type which refers to the number of the map page on which the place or feature appears. Portree is on page **18**.

The figure and letter which follow the page number give the grid rectangle on the map within which the place or feature appears. The grid is formed by the lines of latitude and longitude. The columns are labelled at the top and bottom of the map with a letter and the rows at the sides of the map with a number. Portree is in the grid square where row **2** crosses column **B**.

A

Aalborg ... 57° 2′N 9°54′ E **32 4N**
Aarhus ... 56° 8′N 10°11′ E **32 4P**
Aba ... 5°10′N 7°19′ E **52 2C**
Ābādān ... 30°22′N 48°20′ E **48 3E**
Abakan ... 53°40′N 91°10′ E **41 4K**
ABC Islands ... 12°15′N 69° 0′W **63 5L**
Abeokuta ... 7° 3′N 3°19′ E **52 2B**
Aberdare ... 51°43′N 3°27′W **17 5C**
Aberdare Range ... 0°15′S 36°50′ E **53 3B**
Aberdeen ... 57° 9′N 2° 5′W **18 2F**
Abergavenny ... 51°49′N 3° 1′W **17 5C**
Aberystwyth ... 52°25′N 4° 5′W **17 4B**
Abidjan ... 5°26′N 3°58′W **51 5B**
Abu Dhabi ... 24°28′N 54°22′ E **48 5F**
Abuja ... 9° 5′N 7°32′ E **52 2C**
Acapulco ... 16°51′N 99°55′W **62 4D**
Accra ... 5°35′N 0° 6′W **52 2A**
Accrington ... 53°45′N 2°22′W **16 3D**
Achill Island ... 53°58′N 10° 1′W **19 3A**
Aconcagua ... 32°39′S 70° 0′W **64 7D**
Acre ... 9° 1′S 71° 0′W **66 4A**
Ad Dammām ... 26°20′N 50° 5′ E **48 4F**
Adamawa Highlands 7°20′N 12°20′ E **52 2D**
Adana ... 37° 0′N 35°16′ E **35 4L**
Adare, Cape ... 71° 0′S 171° 0′ E **67 11E**
Addis Ababa ... 9° 2′N 38°42′ E **51 5F**
Adelaide ... 34°52′S 138°30′ E **54 8G**
Adelaide Island ... 67°15′S 68°30′W **67 17D**
Adélie Land ... 68° 0′S 140° 0′ E **67 10D**
Aden ... 12°45′N 45° 0′ E **46 5C**
Aden, Gulf of ... 12°30′N 47°30′ E **46 5C**
Adriatic Sea ... 43° 0′N 16° 0′ E **36 3F**
Ægean Sea ... 38°30′N 25° 0′ E **35 4J**
Aeolian Islands ... 38°30′N 14°57′ E **36 5E**
Afghanistan ■ ... 33° 0′N 65° 0′ E **46 3E**
Africa ... 10° 0′N 20° 0′ E **50 5E**
Agra ... 27°17′N 77°58′ E **46 4F**
Aguascalientes ... 21°53′N 102°18′W **62 3D**
Ahmadabad ... 23° 0′N 72°40′ E **46 4F**
Ahvāz ... 31°20′N 48°40′ E **48 3E**
Ailsa Craig ... 55°15′N 5° 6′W **18 4C**
Aïr ... 18°30′N 8° 0′ E **50 4C**
Airdrie ... 55°52′N 3°57′W **18 4E**
Aire ➜ ... 53°43′N 0°55′W **13 5F**
Aix-en-Provence ... 43°32′N 5°27′ E **33 11L**
Ajaccio ... 41°55′N 8°40′ E **33 12N**
Akita ... 39°45′N 140° 7′ E **45 3D**
Akosombo Dam ... 6°20′N 0° 5′ E **52 2B**
Akron ... 41° 5′N 81°31′W **59 2K**
Aksu ... 41° 5′N 80°10′ E **42 2C**
Al ‘Ayn ... 24°15′N 55°45′ E **48 5G**
Al Aziziyah ... 32°30′N 13° 1′ E **34 5F**
Al Ḩillah ... 32°30′N 44°25′ E **48 3D**
Al Hufūf ... 25°25′N 49°45′ E **48 4E**
Al Jubayl ... 27° 0′N 49°50′ E **48 4E**
Al Kūt ... 32°30′N 46° 0′ E **48 3E**
Al Mubarraz ... 25°30′N 49°40′ E **48 4E**
Alabama ... 33° 0′N 87° 0′W **59 4J**
Alabama ➜ ... 31° 8′N 87°57′W **59 4J**
Alagoas ... 9° 0′S 36° 0′W **66 4H**
Åland Islands ... 60°15′N 20° 0′ E **31 3D**
Alaska ... 64° 0′N 154° 0′W **57 3D**
Alaska, Gulf of ... 58° 0′N 145° 0′W **56 4E**
Alaska Peninsula ... 56° 0′N 159° 0′W **56 4D**
Alaska Range ... 62°50′N 151° 0′W **56 3D**
Albacete ... 39° 0′N 1°50′W **33 13H**
Albania ■ ... 41° 0′N 20° 0′ E **35 3G**
Albany, *Australia* ... 35° 1′S 117°58′ E **54 9C**
Albany, *U.S.A.* ... 42°39′N 73°45′W **59 2M**
Albuquerque ... 35° 5′N 106°39′W **58 3E**
Aldabra Islands ... 9°22′S 46°28′ E **51 6G**
Aldeburgh ... 52°10′N 1°37′ E **17 4H**
Alderney ... 49°42′N 2°11′W **17 7D**
Aleppo ... 36°10′N 37°15′ E **48 2C**
Ålesund ... 62°28′N 6°12′ E **31 3B**
Aleutian Islands ... 52° 0′N 175° 0′W **68 2A**
Alexander Island ... 69° 0′S 70° 0′W **67 17D**
Alexandria ... 31°13′N 29°58′ E **48 3A**
Algarve ... 36°58′N 8°20′W **33 14D**
Algeria ■ ... 28°30′N 2° 0′ E **51 3C**
Algiers ... 36°42′N 3° 8′ E **51 2C**
Alicante ... 38°23′N 0°30′W **33 13H**
Alice Springs ... 23°40′S 133°50′ E **54 6F**
Allahabad ... 25°25′N 81°58′ E **46 4G**
Allegheny Mountains 38°15′N 80°10′W **59 3L**
Allen, Bog of ... 53°15′N 7° 0′W **19 3D**
Allen, Lough ... 54° 8′N 8° 4′W **19 2C**
Alloa ... 56° 7′N 3°47′W **18 3E**
Alma Ata ... 43°15′N 76°57′ E **40 5H**
Almería ... 36°52′N 2°27′W **33 14G**
Alness ... 57°41′N 4°16′W **18 2D**
Alnwick ... 55°24′N 1°42′W **16 1E**
Alps ... 46°30′N 9°30′ E **33 9N**
Altai ... 46°40′N 92°45′ E **40 4J**
Altay ... 47°48′N 88°10′ E **42 2C**
Altun Shan ... 38°30′N 88° 0′ E **42 3C**
Amapá ... 1°40′N 52° 0′W **66 2E**
Amarillo ... 35°13′N 101°50′W **58 3F**
Amazon ➜ ... 0° 5′S 50° 0′W **66 3E**
Amazonas ... 5° 0′S 65° 0′W **66 4B**
Ambon ... 3°43′S 128°12′ E **47 7L**
American Highland ... 73° 0′S 75° 0′ E **67 6E**
American Samoa ... 14°20′S 170° 0′W **55 4S**
Amery Ice Shelf ... 69°30′S 72° 0′ E **67 6D**
Amiens ... 49°54′N 2°16′ E **33 8J**
Amlwch ... 53°24′N 4°20′W **16 3B**
‘Ammān ... 31°57′N 35°52′ E **48 3C**
Amritsar ... 31°35′N 74°57′ E **46 3F**
Amsterdam ... 52°23′N 4°54′ E **32 6L**
Amudarya ➜ ... 43°58′N 59°34′ E **40 5F**
Amundsen Sea ... 72° 0′S 115° 0′W **67 15E**
Amur ➜ ... 52°56′N 141°10′ E **41 4Q**
An Najaf ... 32° 3′N 44°15′ E **48 3D**
An Nāşirīyah ... 31° 0′N 46°15′ E **48 3E**
Anápolis ... 16°15′S 48°50′W **66 6F**
Anatolia ... 39° 0′N 30° 0′ E **48 2B**
Anchorage ... 61°13′N 149°54′W **57 3E**
Ancona ... 43°38′N 13°30′ E **36 3D**
Andalucía ... 37°35′N 5° 0′W **33 14F**
Andaman Islands ... 12°30′N 92°45′ E **46 5H**
Andaman Sea ... 13° 0′N 96° 0′ E **38 7L**
Andes ... 10° 0′S 75°53′W **64 5D**
Andizhan ... 41°10′N 72°15′ E **42 2B**
Andorra ■ ... 42°30′N 1°30′ E **33 11J**
Andover ... 51°12′N 1°29′W **17 5E**
Aneto, Pico de ... 42°37′N 0°40′ E **33 11J**
Angara ➜ ... 58° 5′N 94°20′ E **41 4K**
Angel Falls ... 5°57′N 62°30′W **63 6M**
Angers ... 47°30′N 0°35′W **33 9H**
Anglesey ... 53°17′N 4°20′W **16 3B**
Angola ■ ... 12° 0′S 18° 0′ E **51 7D**
Angoulême ... 45°39′N 0°10′ E **33 10J**
Angus ... 56°46′N 2°56′W **15 3E**
Ankara ... 39°57′N 32°54′ E **35 4K**
Annaba ... 36°50′N 7°46′ E **34 4E**
Annan ... 54°59′N 3°16′W **18 5E**
Annan ➜ ... 54°58′N 3°16′W **18 4E**
Annapolis ... 38°59′N 76°30′W **59 3L**
Annobón ... 1°25′S 5°36′ E **50 6C**
Anshan ... 41° 5′N 122°58′ E **43 2G**
Antalya ... 36°52′N 30°45′ E **35 4K**
Antananarivo ... 18°55′S 47°31′ E **51 7G**
Antarctic Peninsula ... 67° 0′S 60° 0′W **67 18D**
Antarctica ... 90° 0′S 0° 0′W **67 3F**
Antigua & Barbuda ■ 17°20′N 61°48′W **63 4M**
Antofagasta ... 23°50′S 70°30′W **65 6D**
Antrim ... 54°43′N 6°14′W **19 2E**
Antrim, Mountains of 55° 3′N 6°14′W **19 2E**
Antwerp ... 51°13′N 4°25′ E **32 7L**
Anvers Island ... 64°30′S 63°40′W **67 17D**
Aomori ... 40°45′N 140°45′ E **45 2D**
Aoraki Mount Cook ... 43°36′S 170° 9′ E **55 10P**
Apennines ... 44°30′N 10° 0′ E **36 3D**
Apia ... 13°50′S 171°50′W **55 4S**
Appalachian Mountains ... 38° 0′N 80° 0′W **59 3K**
Appleby-in-Westmorland ... 54°35′N 2°29′W **16 2D**
Aqaba ... 29°31′N 35° 0′ E **48 4C**
Arabia ... 25° 0′N 45° 0′ E **38 6F**
Arabian Sea ... 16° 0′N 65° 0′ E **46 5E**
Aracaju ... 10°55′S 37° 4′W **66 5H**
Araçatuba ... 21°10′S 50°30′W **66 7E**
Araguaia ➜ ... 5°21′S 48°41′W **66 4F**
Arāk ... 34° 0′N 49°40′ E **48 3E**
Araks ➜ ... 40° 5′N 48°29′ E **48 1E**
Aral Sea ... 45° 0′N 58°20′ E **40 5F**
Aran Islands ... 53° 6′N 9°38′W **19 3B**
Ararat, Mount ... 39°50′N 44°15′ E **48 2D**
Arbroath ... 56°34′N 2°35′W **18 3F**
Arctic Ocean ... 78° 0′N 160° 0′W **67 18B**
Ardabīl ... 38°15′N 48°18′ E **48 2E**
Ardnamurchan, Point of ... 56°43′N 6°14′W **18 3B**
Ardrossan ... 55°39′N 4°49′W **18 4D**
Ards Peninsula ... 54°33′N 5°34′W **19 2F**
Arequipa ... 16°20′S 71°30′W **65 5D**
Argentina ■ ... 35° 0′S 66° 0′W **65 7E**
Argun ➜ ... 53°20′N 121°28′ E **43 1F**
Argyle, Lake ... 16°20′S 128°40′ E **54 5E**
Argyll ... 56°10′N 5°20′W **18 3C**
Argyll & Bute ... 56°13′N 5°28′W **15 3D**
Arica ... 18°32′S 70°20′W **65 5D**
Aripuanã ➜ ... 5° 7′S 60°25′W **66 4C**
Arizona ... 34° 0′N 112° 0′W **58 4D**
Arkaig, Loch ... 56°59′N 5°10′W **18 3C**
Arkansas ... 35° 0′N 92°30′W **59 4H**
Arkansas ➜ ... 33°47′N 91° 4′W **59 4H**
Arkhangelsk ... 64°38′N 40°36′ E **31 3J**
Arklow ... 52°48′N 6°10′W **19 4E**
Armagh ... 54°21′N 6°39′W **19 2E**
Armenia ■ ... 40°20′N 45° 0′ E **48 1D**
Arnhem ... 51°58′N 5°55′ E **32 7L**
Arnhem Land ... 13°10′S 134°30′ E **54 4F**
Arran ... 55°34′N 5°12′W **18 4C**
Arranmore ... 55° 0′N 8°30′W **19 1C**
Aru Islands ... 6° 0′S 134°30′ E **47 7M**
Aruba ... 12°30′N 70° 0′W **63 5L**
Arusha ... 3°20′S 36°40′ E **53 3B**
Arvayheer ... 46°15′N 102°48′ E **42 2E**
As Sulaymānīyah, *Iraq* ... 35°35′N 45°29′ E **48 2E**
As Sulaymānīyah, *Saudi Arabia* ... 24° 9′N 47°18′ E **48 5E**
Asahikawa ... 43°46′N 142°22′ E **45 2D**
Asamankese ... 5°50′N 0°40′W **52 2A**
Ascension Island ... 7°57′S 14°23′W **51 6A**
Ashford ... 51° 8′N 0°53′ E **17 5G**
Ashington ... 55°11′N 1°33′W **16 1E**
Ashkhabad ... 37°58′N 58°24′ E **48 2G**
Ashton under Lyne ... 53°29′N 2° 6′W **16 3D**
Asmara ... 15°19′N 38°55′ E **51 4F**
Assam ... 26° 0′N 93° 0′ E **46 4H**
Astana ... 51°10′N 71°30′ E **40 4H**
Astrakhan ... 46°25′N 48° 5′ E **38 5E**
Asunción ... 25°10′S 57°30′W **65 6F**
Aswân ... 24° 4′N 32°57′ E **48 5B**
Asyût ... 27°11′N 31° 4′ E **48 4B**
Aţ Tā’if ... 21° 5′N 40°27′ E **48 5D**
Atacama Desert ... 24° 0′S 69°20′W **64 6E**
Athens ... 37°58′N 23°43′ E **35 4H**
Athlone ... 53°25′N 7°56′W **19 3D**
Athy ... 53° 0′N 7° 0′W **19 4E**
Atlanta ... 33°45′N 84°23′W **59 4K**
Atlantic Ocean ... 0° 0′ 20° 0′W **68 3G**
Atlas Mountains ... 32°30′N 5° 0′W **50 2B**
Auckland ... 36°52′S 174°46′ E **55 9P**
Augsburg ... 48°25′N 10°52′ E **33 8P**
Augusta ... 44°19′N 69°47′W **59 2N**
Austin ... 30°17′N 97°45′W **58 4G**
Australia ■ ... 23° 0′S 135° 0′ E **54 6D**
Australian Capital Territory (A.C.T.) ... 35°30′S 149° 0′ E **54 9J**
Austria ■ ... 47° 0′N 14° 0′ E **34 2F**
Aviemore ... 57°12′N 3°50′W **18 2E**
Avignon ... 43°57′N 4°50′ E **33 11L**
Avon ➜, *Bristol* ... 51°29′N 2°41′W **17 5D**
Avon ➜, *Dorset* ... 50°44′N 1°46′W **17 6E**
Avon ➜, *Warwickshire* ... 52° 0′N 2° 8′W **17 4D**
Awe, Loch ... 56°17′N 5°16′W **18 3C**
Ayers Rock = Uluru ... 25°23′S 131° 5′ E **54 7F**
Aylesbury ... 51°49′N 0°49′W **17 5F**
Ayr ... 55°28′N 4°38′W **18 4D**
Azerbaijan ■ ... 40°20′N 48° 0′ E **48 1E**
Azores ... 38° 0′N 27° 0′W **68 3H**
Azov, Sea of ... 46° 0′N 36°30′ E **35 2L**